Practical Procurement

by

R J Carter MA FRSA MCIPS MCMI Cert Ed
and
S K Kirby BA (Hons) MCIPS MCMI Dip.M Cert Ed

Practical Procurement

First edition published by Cambridge Academic, The Studio, High Green, Gt. Shelford, Cambridge CB2 5EG.

ISBN 1-903-49925-9

Cambridge Academic

Imprints include:
Liverpool Academic Press
Liverpool Business Publishing
Tudor Educational

Table of Contents

Foreword

This is a procurement textbook that does not attempt to compete with, or cover the same ground, to any extent, that existing procurement textbooks cover. Rather, we have taken the view that a text was needed to provide what might be termed a detailed overview of and introduction to, the fundamentals of procurement.

Our hope is that this text will serve as an introduction to procurement studies for students of the new CIPS level 3 and level 4 qualifications as well as for students of procurement option modules on courses such as BTEC Higher Business Studies. We have covered many of the basics of procurement such as tendering and supplier selection and general procurement methods such as the use of 'call-off' orders and negotiation – staple fare for any procurement text. Additionally, however, we have tried to introduce students to some of the newer aspects of procurement such as eProcurement.

Whilst focusing on the fundamentals of procurement we have, nevertheless, attempted to provide an introduction to some of the more strategic aspects of procurement, some of which are the topics of much discussion in general business circles and in particular, procurement circles, today. These are topics such as strategic partnerships, outsourcing and the purchasing of services and purchasing ethics. There is much discussion today about the merits, or otherwise, of entering into strategic partnerships with suppliers, a discussion that we hope to have contributed to. Outsourcing is an aspect of procurement that is becoming more and more important as organisations seek to outsource more and more services and as organisations spend more and more on goods and services, in terms of percentage of turnover or budget, the focus on purchasing ethics becomes ever greater.

The main focus of this text is on procurement but we have also attempted to provide an introduction to some of the ancillary aspects of supply chain operations and management such as logistics, including international logistics – increasingly important in these times of globalisation.

Lastly, we have provided an introduction to a concept that is becoming more recognised and well known, that of relationships. Here, we have looked at both internal relationships and external ones, the view being that buyers must be aware of these relationships, how maintaining sound relationships both internally and externally can be of benefit to the buying organisation. There is also the need to attempt to select the 'right' type of relationship to suit different procurement situations.

We are grateful to the copyright holders of material that has been included and specific acknowledgements have been made at appropriate points in the text.

Ray Carter
Steve Kirby

Consultants' Biographies

R J Carter MA FRSA MCIPS MCMI Cert Ed

Ray is the Director of DPSS Consultants, (Developing People Serving the Supply Chain), which is an international training and development consultancy made up of 20 specialist consultants. He began his management career in the public sector and thereafter for a large food manufacturer in the UK. He graduated from Thames Polytechnic with a Masters Degree in Management Studies in 1981.

His first book related to supply chain management was published in 1982 and has become a recommended text for a number of courses, including The Chartered Institute of Purchasing and Supply. This was followed by other titles, including People and Organisations and Policy Planning and Organisation. His latest title is *Understanding Supply Chains*, co-edited with Professor David Jessop. Ray has had numerous articles and papers published in journals such as Supply Management and the Center for Advanced Procurement's Praxis publication. Ray is also Chairman of the Procurement Best Practice Forum, which is made up of many large blue-chip organisations, the purpose of which is to identify and disseminate supply chain management best practices.

Until 1991 Ray was Principal Lecturer in Supply Chain Management at the Business School, University of North London. In recent years, he has undertaken training and consultancy assignments for organisations such as Shell, Lucas Engineering and Systems, the Chartered Institute of Purchasing and Supply, BRC, Nederlandse Aardolie Maatschappij.B.V, Abu Dhabi Company for Onshore Oil Operations (ADCO), UK Intervention Board, Ericsson, British Aerospace, Marconi, BBC, Magnox, Ordnance Survey, ChevronTexaco and Shell International BV. Ray has worked in many locations, including the Far East, the Middle East, South America, Europe and Africa. The majority of these events have been related to strategic issues in relation to supply chain management and procurement.

S K Kirby BA (Hons) MCIPS MCMI Dip M Cert Ed

Steve is a self-employed Supply Chain trainer and consultant. His early purchasing and supply career was spent working in a purchasing capacity for a number of companies in the West Midlands all involved in the heavy engineering sector. From 1979 until 2002 he was a senior lecturer at Sandwell College in the West Midlands and specialised in teaching all levels of CIPS provision from Certificate level up to Graduate Diploma. His particular specialisation was 'pure' purchasing modules with Stores and Inventory subjects as a secondary specialisation. From 1990 onwards, he was programme manager of CIPS courses aimed both at part-time and full-time students, the latter courses providing Steve with much experience of students from overseas, particularly from Arab countries and sub-Saharan Africa.

Steve is currently a visiting lecturer at Thames Valley University, teaching CIPS programmes at both Foundation and Professional levels. He is chief examiner for the CIPS Advanced Certificate module of Preparing and Managing Contracts and acts as a 'contract' examination invigilator for CIPS.

Steve is Senior Purchasing Tutor for Cheltenham Tutorial College. In this last capacity, he gives distance learning support to students at all levels of CIPS provision and has written study materials for the college. In recent years, Steve has had articles published on the 'Students' page of 'Supply Management' (CIPS journal).

Steve has also recently provided supply chain training in the private sector for Consignia (now Royal Mail) and has carried out CIPS-related training, on behalf of DPSS, for ShellExpro Ltd. in both Nigeria and Aberdeen. He has also provided CILT training for BMMI Ltd. in Bahrain and has recently completed an ongoing contract involving interviewing NHS supplies staff, in various parts of the UK, to identify training needs on behalf of PASA.

Steve also acts as a private tutor for school students specialising in general business studies, French and History.

1.   Fundamentals of Procurement

Introduction

Effective procurement can affect an organisation's profitability. It brings together customers and suppliers for the purpose of delighting the end customer.

Definitions of Procurement

'Procurement is the process that involves the design, specification and acquisition of goods and services.'

'A critical business process that enables an organisaton to secure a wide range of externally provided resource, (and value), efficiently and effectively, from need to disposal'

Our definition is designed to highlight the 'inclusive' nature of procurement in modern business organisations. The reference to a wide range of resources is designed to emphasise that procurement, as a process, covers everything from simple stationery contracts to complex outsourcing projects for critical strategic business services, like IT support.

The reference to 'value' is meant to highlight that often, extra added value can be gained from the marketplace in the form of new technology, methodology innovations and market development. All of these are examples of the value that can be obtained by careful exploitation of market forces.

5 Key Procurement Questions

From a very practical point of view, procurement professionals (and their customers) face many fundamental questions about procurement, some of which are affected by the organisational context and the nature of what is being sourced. We have identified five key questions, which are:

- What are we trying to secure?

- What is really Fit for our Purpose?

- Who should provide the resource?

- What are the risks/ rewards?

- What is the correct procurement methodology?

In many respects, how these questions are addressed has a very significant impact on the subsequent success of any procurement project or activity. Most of the failures to really 'secure' the resource have their origins in a failure to recognise the importance of these questions.

The reference to 'criticality' is designed to highlight the importance of the process to every type of organisation, public or private, civil or military, funded or charity based.

Objectives of procurement

The following should be the key objectives of any world class procurement organisation.

- Support and contribute to the successful fulfilment of the organisation's corporate objectives.

- Secure resources.

- Understand and exploit the market place.

- Co-operate, liaise and communicate with customer organisations.

- Act as a conduit for innovation and added value.

- Provide the discipline required to manage all costs.

Traditional v New Age Procurement

It is interesting to compare and contrast the priorities and conventions of traditional versus new age/world class procurement, see table below:

Traditional	New Age/World Class
Price	Total Cost of Ownership (TCO)
Adversarial	Collaborative
Late Supplier Involvement (LSI)	Early Supplier Involvement (ESI)
Prescriptive specifications	Performance
Quality control	Quality assurance
Inspection	Prevention
Acceptable Quality Levels (AQL)	Total Quality Management (TQM)
Just in Case (JIC)	Just in Time (JIT)
Contract based	Performance based
Win/lose	Win/win
Many suppliers	Few suppliers
Gatekeepers	Facilitators

Concept of Total Cost of Ownership vs Price

Many buyers and procurement people still take a traditional view of what is important in procurement, and tend to focus on paying the lowest possible price for the items they purchase. Such people take the view that, if they can be seen to pay the lowest price, they are obtaining the best value. In recent years, this view has been challenged, and the prevailing view among experts now is that buyers should seek to obtain the lowest TCO for the following reasons:

☐ Price is often a poor measure of value.

☐ Procurement is a total process and each stage has a cost.

☐ There is the concept of added value.

☐ There is the concept of cost + time.

TCO is, therefore, not necessarily the same thing as the lowest price, and may be defined as price plus one or more of the following:

☐ **Inspection costs** – a more expensive supplier whose products require less inspection than those of a cheaper supplier may give a lower TCO. The cost of inspection may be calculated easily by multiplying the time needed for inspection by the wage rate for this job.

☐ **Rectification costs** – again, a supplier whose work needs frequent rectification is likely to be more expensive than one whose products, even though more expensive, do not.

☐ **Lost production time** – a cheap supplier whose service lets buyers down and causes production line or operation stoppages due to late deliveries is, in reality, considerably more expensive than one whose service is on time all the time.

☐ **Holding 'just-in-case' stock** – the cost of holding such stock, owing to having a supplier whose service is erratic, needs to be added to the purchase price. A supplier who can give 'just in time' service can save much expense by enabling your stockholding costs to be reduced.

☐ **Missed innovation opportunities** – a supplier who is only able to supply what is required without being able to offer innovation is likely to hold the buyer's company back in terms of satisfying or delighting its customers. Suppliers able to be proactive in terms of suggesting innovations can help the buyer's company keep ahead of its rivals.

☐ **Purchase, progress, accounts and administration costs** – suppliers who have outdated systems for coping with these aspects of business will add to total costs. Suppliers who are capable of working with up-to-date technology and who are able to use electronic means of transmitting information, data, documents, etc. will help make the buyer's operation more streamlined and reduce operating costs.

☐ **Communication costs** – suppliers who are capable of working without being 'chased' frequently will help reduce this aspect of cost.

Food for Thought

How often do you focus on achieving lowest TCO in your job? What extra savings could you achieve if you did focus more on lowest TCO?

Definition of Total Cost of Ownership

'The total cost of ownership is more than simply price, and has a bearing on developing the wider role of procurement into total cost management. It is the total you actually pay for goods and services, including such things as tooling, duty, inventory-carrying costs, inspection, remedy or rectification and so on. It is an obvious fact, yet a commonly ignored one, that a low price may lead to a high total cost of ownership.'

Total cost of ownership needs to be considered for all purchases. When the purchase of a piece of capital equipment is being considered and quotations from a number of suppliers are being analysed, consideration of relative total costs of ownership can help the buyer decide which supplier to use. Total cost of ownership includes the following criteria.

- **Business need** – the item being offered must meet our requirements.
- **Design** – the ability of the item to perform in the way we want.
- **Specification** – particular features that one supplier's product may have that another does not.
- **Acquisition** – what are the relative costs of acquisition?
- **Commission** – the commissioning of capital items can be expensive. Comparisons should be made between potential suppliers.
- **Storage** – costs of items needing to be stored prior to use.
- **Use** – how much is it likely to cost to use the item in terms of consumables, energy, etc. Comparisons can be made between potential suppliers.
- **Maintenance** – the cost of servicing and repairs as well as potential costs of spare parts. Service intervals can be projected and compared between potential suppliers.
- **Disposal** – how much is it likely to cost to dispose of the item at the end of its projected life span?

The Procurement Cycle

Definition

'The totality of events, in sequence, that make up the main part of the activity of purchasing, from original identification of the need, to payment of the invoice in respect of the goods/services purchased to satisfy the need.'

The activities that make up the procurement cycle need to be considered. These are the activities, in the order in which they take place, that are required to complete a purchase successfully. For repeat purchases, some of these activities, for example enquiry/quotation, may be omitted.

- Need.

- Business case.

- Specification and quality assurance.

- Sourcing.

- Cost and price analysis.

- Supplier selection.

- Negotiation/bid evaluation.

- Contract award.

- Delivery.

- Payment to Vendor rating

Today, all these activities, where they involve communication, can be done electronically. An issue of great importance is the creation of an audit trail so that such matters as the justification for making the purchase can always be checked.

To this end, once the system has been accessed at some point, there should be a means of cross-referencing all the other stages in the cycle. For example, once a purchase order has been accessed, it should be possible, from cross-references contained in it, to access the original requisition and any enquiry and quotation work that has preceded it.

The Role of the Customer and Supplier

The Customer

At first sight it might appear that the customer does not have any role to play in purchases that are made. However, it is important that there is a focus on end customer requirements at all times so that the buyer's company is able to 'delight its customer'. To this end, the customer can provide information that will assist in this process such as:

☐ Specific requirements in terms of design/specification and any special features required.

☐ Any changes in specification over time.

☐ Up-to-date demand information.

The Supplier

Suppliers must always fulfil the requirements of the end customer in terms of price, quality and service and any other details that may be contained in the contract, for example, after-sales service. This will include any special requirements that the end customer may have, such as specific delivery requirements. It is important also to make sure that any changes in end customer requirements are communicated to suppliers as quickly as possible.

Impact upon profit

Sound procurement can have a great impact upon a company's profitability. This is achieved by making savings in total cost of ownership rather than merely in terms of purchase price. Any savings made go directly onto the 'bottom line'. This can be illustrated as shown in figure 1.

Figure 1

The original situation shows the value of purchased goods and services at about 50% of turnover. In some companies this figure could be as high as 80% although, in some sectors of the economy, it is likely to be smaller.

☐ Total 'pie' = total sales revenue (turnover).

Figure 2

Figure 2 shows the situation after a saving is made in the value of purchased goods and services. Just how great the procurement department's contribution to profitability can be may be illustrated as follows.

Total sales - £200m	Total purchases - £100m	Profit - £20m
£200m	£95m (5% reduction)	£25m (25% increase)

This example gives a 1:5 ratio of savings to profit increase and is known as the 'profit leverage effect'.

Food for thought

Is the Procurement Department in your organisation considered to be able to make a strategic contribution to profitability?

Chapter Summary

Some of the most fundamental elements of procurement have now been considered:

- ☐ The concept of total cost of ownership and how it differs from mere consideration of purchase price, and how real savings may be generated by reducing them.

- ☐ The range of activities that comprise the job of procurement, their sequence and importance.

- ☐ How both customer and supplier can help up in the ongoing process of 'delighting the customer' and how information from the customer is particularly useful and important in this regard.

- ☐ The contribution that sound procurement can make to a company's profitability. All commercial organisations seek profit, and procurement can play a major part in its achievement.

Case Study

Fleet Contracting

Fleet Plc is a large manufacturing company producing oil and gas products for the UK and overseas market. The Company's procurement function has the reputation of being very aggressive with contractors, and is noted for its ability to achieve the lowest prices paid in the Industry. One of the critical items sourced by Fleet is the special packaging used in almost all of its products. The packaging contract for this key item is placed yearly, and the company have used a number of suppliers in the past, including some from Mexico. The negotiating team spend a great deal of time and effort evaluating the relative merits of each bid that comes in. The head of Procurement, Mary Finley, feels that the main objective is to "force the contractors into reducing their prices".

The annual contracting process for this item has taken on great importance in the Contracting office. Everybody knows that it involves a lot of extra work. The administrative staff have to spend time revising their records to accommodate the new supplier. The Procurement staff are also involved in this process, new stock control systems have to be established storage and coding systems often need adjusting. The head of Quality Control likes to spend time with the new supplier, so that they are completely familiar with Fleet's quality control Systems. As the Procurement manager states: "We always encounter teething problems when the packaging contract is awarded to a new supplier, in fact it's a nightmare, but the price saving must make it worthwhile". Recently an important Value Analysis project was postponed due to the pressure of work placed on procurement by this complex contracting ritual.

The contract for this year was awarded to small company located in West Africa, the team spent several days negotiating with the contractor and inspecting their plant before signing the contract. Their prices were very competitive, up to 10% lower than the nearest rival, a local UK company. The managing director of Fleet is very pleased: "Every penny we save on unit price falls through to the bottom line as profit. That's what I call effective contracting".

Tasks

1. How would you evaluate Fleet's contracting policy?

2. How could you go about calculating the total cost of securing this resource?

3. What are the risks associated with their approach to procurement?

2. Specification Process

Introduction

There are a number of different types of specification commonly used in industry and commerce. Many organisations develop a team approach towards specification development and involve both suppliers and customers at an early stage. This is known as 'Early Supplier Involvement', or ESI.

Importance of Effective Specification Development

Definitions of specification

'A document that prescribes the requirements with which the product or service has to conform. A specification should refer to or include drawings, patterns or other relevant documents and should also indicate the means and the criteria whereby conformity can be checked.'

International Standards Organisation (ISO)

'Specifications are meant to communicate our requirements to the supplier and not confuse them.'

or

'Detailed description of any item/service'

This definition is, perhaps, more of a 'working definition' and includes the following functions of a technical specification.

- It provides the purchaser's requirements – a specification tells suppliers and other stakeholders exactly what the buyer requires. In most industrial and commercial situations, particularly those concerned with engineering applications, requirements are exact, not an approximation. Properly developed specifications clearly indicate the exact nature of the buyer's requirements, often incorporating dimensions and tolerances.

- It allows comparison of supply market competition – once a specification has been developed, it may be disseminated to as many potential suppliers as is thought necessary as the basis of a request for quotation (RFQ). Subsequent quotations received may then be compared by the buyer to identify the 'best' supplier.

- It forms the basis of a contract – the specification will usually form the basis of the purchase order given to the chosen supplier and, as such, will also form the basis of a legally-binding contract. There will usually be terms of the contract contained in the purchase order relating to specific aspects of the specification.

Food for thought

Does your organisation have a standard definition of a specification that demonstrates not only what it is but also how it is used? If so, what is it?

It should be clear, from the above, that the development of effective specifications is extremely important. This is because of the need to obtain exactly what is required, the need to source the supply market to obtain the best deal or best value, and the need to bind suppliers in terms of a contractual obligation to supply exactly what is required.

One way in which procurement can be allowed to contribute to achieving best value is if specifications are developed with variety control in mind. This may be defined as:

'The selection of the optimum number of sizes or types of products, processes or services to meet prevailing needs'.

If an unnecessary number of varieties of materials and spares is allowed to proliferate, procurement loses its ability and scope to utilise economies of scale when making purchases.

Types of Specification

> **Food for thought**
>
> Do the specifications used in your organisation satisfy the above criteria? If not, why not?

There are many different types of specification in common use commercially, as follows.

Brand name

Advantages – They are simple and quick to use because no development is required and they will also guarantee consistency of quality from one purchase to the next.

Disadvantages – They negate supply market competition.

Sample

Advantages – They are easy and quick to give to or receive from suppliers (depending on who has the sample).

Disadvantages – It is not always easy to determine the content of a sample and there may be an issue regarding consistency with the sample of the bulk of the items. In other words, if the supplier has made the sample (rather than it being given to the supplier by the buyer), a great deal of effort may have been put into making a really good one and the bulk may not be up to the same standard. There is also the issue of the cost of producing a sample and the question of who bears the cost.

Design

Usually represented by a drawing or series of drawings.

Advantages – Because the design will be produced by the buyer's company, there will be adequate control over it and it should reflect exactly the buyer's company's requirements.

Disadvantages – Such designs are costly to produce and there is the risk that, if the item when supplied does not perform in the manner expected, providing the supplier has supplied exactly in accordance with the design, the legal risk is borne by the buyer's company.

Standards

These are published standards such as ISO and EuroNorms.

Advantages – Low cost. Standards are readily available from the relevant standards authority at low cost and, often, it is only necessary to quote the relevant standard number to the supplier for them to understand exactly what is required. If the supplier is not familiar with the specific standard, it can always be looked up.

Disadvantages – The use of standards may be seen to limit innovation because of their perceived rigidity. It is also important to ensure that up-to-date standards are always used, because they do change over time.

Performance

This is a specification where the supplier is told only what performance is required from the item, rather than how to make it.

Advantages – These specifications, growing in popularity, require a high degree of supplier input and, as such, are seen to utilise the supplier's expertise and to induce a greater sense of commitment to the project by the supplier because they are putting their name to the design of the item. Also, from the buyer's company's viewpoint, the cost of producing the design is transferred to the supplier (although this may be passed back to the buyer later) and time is not committed to the design work by the buyer's company.

Disadvantages – There is the risk of loss of control of the design process and subsequent quality of the product supplied. There is also the risk of the supplier designing the item in a manner that 'ties' the buyer to the supplier.

Description

This is usually a simple written document describing what is required.

Advantages – It is easy, quick and simple to write (it is not really suitable for describing highly complex items).

Disadvantages – There may be errors both in the writing of the description itself or in its interpretation by the supplier.

The advantages and disadvantages of these types of specification are summarised in the following table.

Methods	Advantages	Disadvantages
Brand	Simple, quick	Competition
Sample	Easy, quick	Content Consistency
Design	Control	Costly and risk, time
Standards	Low cost	Limits innovation
Performance	Supplier input, time, costs	Loss of control
Description	Easy, quick, simple	Errors

Food for thought

Does your organisation favour any of the above specifications? If so, why?

Team Approach to Specifications

It is widely believed that, in order to develop effective specifications, a 'team' approach is required. A further definition of specifications will help to illustrate this idea:

'Specifications are the most detailed method of describing requirements. They are the descriptions that tell the supplier exactly what the buyer wants to purchase. Because they impinge extensively on the activities of engineering, operations, procurement and quality, optimum specifications vitally influence the contribution made by all these departments to the organisation's success.'

It can be seen that an effective specification requires a compromise involving a number of basic objectives, each relating to a particular department in a company

☐ Engineering requirements of design purpose and quality. The item must be capable of doing the job for which it is intended, and must be reliable.

☐ Production requirements for ease of manufacture by the supplier. The item designed must be capable of being produced in a straightforward/cost-effective manner.

☐ Procurement requirements of availability and cost-effective purchase. The item must be capable not only of being purchased, but also of being purchased cost-effectively. In other words, ideally, it will be designed so as to be readily available from a number of sources although it should be recognised that this may not always be possible.

These sometimes conflicting views need to be reconciled if a specification is to be truly successful. There are a number of methods of achieving this reconciliation, although it should be noted that there is no one 'right' approach.

☐ **Informal approach** – this recognises the right of procurement staff to challenge designs on an 'ad-hoc' basis if it is felt that some modification would give greater availability or cost-effectiveness. Marketing would also have the same right regarding customer attractiveness.

☐ **Formal committee approach** – a design committee is set up with representatives from all interested departments, and no new design is passed unless accepted by all members. Like all committees this may become unwieldy and time-consuming and may lead to unresolved arguments.

☐ **Procurement co-ordinator** – this involves a person experienced both in engineering and commercial disciplines who reviews designs for commercial implications as they leave the drawing board and modifies them, as necessary, if technical considerations cause commercial problems. This is a very structured and expensive approach and is not widely used.

Food for thought

Do you recognise the 'compromise' between basic departmental objectives referred to above? If so, how does your organisation reconcile them?

The Use of Performance Specifications

Performance specifications were introduced earlier. They are seen by many buyers and procurement companies as being the way forward because they are perceived to have the following advantages.

☐ They are total – the supplier is responsible for providing/ specifying the whole item/product including sub-assemblies and individual parts.

☐ They use supplier input – they call upon the supplier's expertise and knowledge of the product to arrive at a suitable design. In effect, they say to the supplier 'you are the expert in this area, provide something that will do the job we require'.

☐ They give an assured quality level – if the supplier assures the buyer that the item will perform as required and, in the event, they do not, the supplier may legally be held liable (assuming the contract is drafted to include such a stipulation).

☐ They usually allow faster delivery time to market – owing to greater levels of expertise, the supplier will usually be able to complete designs faster than the buyer's company would be able to. This will allow faster time to market (the time elapsing between the need being established and the goods actually being available to customers). This may give a company significant competitive edge.

ESI and ECI Concepts

Early Supplier Involvement (ESI)

In recent years there has been a marked increase in the use of this technique. It relates to the involvement of tried and trusted suppliers in the provision of items/ products. The concept is sometimes known as Bilateral Design Process, and the following definition explains it further:

'World class companies gain from increasing willingness of their suppliers to come up with innovations and cost saving suggestions and to work collaboratively. The system replaces a vicious circle of mistrust with a virtuous circle of co-operation.'

The idea is to utilise suppliers' expertise at the 'design' stage of products, and to seek contributions from suppliers based on best practice, innovation and proactivity on an ongoing basis through the life cycle of the product. ESI can reasonably be taken together with performance specifications, because the idea of both is to stimulate contributions from the supplier. Contributions may be in the form of technical suggestions related to the actual design or operation of the product/item, or ones related to cost implications and issues of best value.

The advantage of ESI to the buyer is to gain from the supplier's experience and expertise, and to have a supplier who is more committed to the project than might otherwise be the case because the supplier is 'buying into' the success of the project. The supplier effectively becomes a 'stakeholder' in the project. The advantage of ESI to the supplier is that it commits the buyer to them to a large extent, and means that they should continue to gain business over time.

There are perceived to be some disadvantages of ESI from the buyer's viewpoint.

- It may have the effect of 'tying' the buyer to a supplier that proves to be unsatisfactory in the long term although they might appear satisfactory at the outset. This can be particularly true where the supplier takes on most or all of the design effort.

- There can be a question over intellectual property rights. The supplier may want to reserve the right to use the design for other customers, an idea to which the buyer may object. In this event, much negotiation/clarification of rights may be required and the resulting agreement incorporated into the contract between buyer and seller.

- There may be a question of which party bears the costs if the design ultimately does not work satisfactorily or is not attractive to customers. Again, much negotiation may be necessary to settle such a dispute.

For these reasons, it is generally advised that ESI be considered only with tried and tested, trustworthy suppliers.

Food for thought

Is ESI employed in your organisation? If not, is there any scope for it in your opinion?

Early Customer Involvement (ECI)

Definition

'The involvement of the internal customer in the procurement process with a view to incorporating customer requirements so that these requirements may be satisfied or exceeded.'

The idea here is to gain as much information as possible about internal customers' requirements, the view being that customer requirements may best be satisfied if the members of the supply chain know what they are. Customer requirements may be:

☐　　　Technical, relating to product features or how the product performs.

☐　　　Related to actual demand and demand patterns/changes.

☐　　　Related to customer perceptions of best value.

The view is that, if members of the supply chain have a thorough knowledge of issues such as those above, they will be better placed than otherwise to satisfy the customer's requirements or even exceed them ('delight the customer').

This concept may appear to be similar to the well-established practice of Marketing and Market Research, but where customers are businesses themselves, ECI concerns involving internal customers in the actual design process so that contributions may be made directly.

A formalised method of ECI is known as the 'House of Quality'. This involves matching customer requirements against technical features of the product, and also involves using suppliers' contributions and attempting to match these to customer requirements. In order to be able to view these various contributions and match them effectively a matrix format is often used, as follows:

Value Analysis (VA) and Value Engineering (VE)

When specifications are considered, it is always useful to think in terms of the specification being written in a manner designed to allow the lowest total cost of ownership. To this end, VA and VE can contribute to specifications by allowing an organisation to consider cost reduction.

Food for thought

Does your organisation employ ECI? If not, is there any scope for it?

Definitions

Value analysis – is a systematic procedure aimed at ensuring that necessary functions are achieved at minimum costs without detriment to quality, reliability, performance and delivery.

Value engineering – this is the application of value analysis at the pre-production and development stage.

Both VA and VE, therefore, are aimed at:

    ☐   cost reduction.

    ☐   maintaining performance, reliability, marketability.

    ☐   improvements in working practices, waste reduction.

    ☐   standardisation – it is important, at all times, to ensure that the proliferation of an unnecessary variety of materials is avoided.

The VA process is a logical, systematic approach to removing unnecessary cost from products or processes, that moves through a planned sequence of events, illustrated by the following elements of the study.

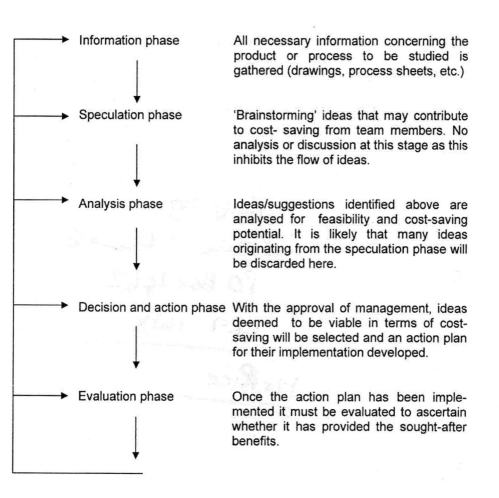

Information phase — All necessary information concerning the product or process to be studied is gathered (drawings, process sheets, etc.)

Speculation phase — 'Brainstorming' ideas that may contribute to cost- saving from team members. No analysis or discussion at this stage as this inhibits the flow of ideas.

Analysis phase — Ideas/suggestions identified above are analysed for feasibility and cost-saving potential. It is likely that many ideas originating from the speculation phase will be discarded here.

Decision and action phase — With the approval of management, ideas deemed to be viable in terms of cost-saving will be selected and an action plan for their implementation developed.

Evaluation phase — Once the action plan has been implemented it must be evaluated to ascertain whether it has provided the sought-after benefits.

The benefits and objectives of VA may be summarised by considering VA and the steps of the VA process.

☐ Identification of unnecessary costs, e.g. materials, methods, standards, specifications (anything that does not contribute to design features, reliability, performance or customer attractiveness).

☐ Elimination of unnecessary costs – removing such aspects identified above from the specification.

☐ Questioning of components, methods and materials, e.g. asking questions of a specification such as 'Is this feature necessary? Does it contribute anything positive to the process?'

☐ Organising a procedure/framework but encouraging creative thinking, e.g. the brainstorming process.

☐ Stressing the importance of the decision and action and evaluation phases.

VA is usually conducted on a team basis with representatives from all interested departments attending meetings. Which departments are represented will depend on the organisation, but typically, representatives from the technical functions, estimating and procurement would be part of the team. It would be useful to consider procurement's contribution to VA:

☐ **ESI** – suppliers may have useful contributions to make. Procurement can elicit these.

☐ **Review of fitness for purpose/specifications**. Procurement staff, taking a non-technical view of specifications, can make suggestions that may have escaped the attention of technical staff.

☐ **Market intelligence**. Procurement staff can make contributions to the process based on knowledge of supply markets, market conditions and new processes/materials.

☐ **Logistical issues, etc**. VA does not focus merely on specifications. If savings can be made in such areas as transportation, packaging and inventory, procurement staff should be well placed to make such contributions.

☐ **Facilitation**. Many of the results of the VA process will have to be implemented by and through co-operation with suppliers. Procurement has a major role in ensuring that this takes place.

Specific outcomes of Value Analysis will depend on the specific organisation and products/processes that are the subject of the analysis process but, typically, will include:

☐ alternative materials.

☐ simple design.

☐ reduction in material content.

☐ computer aided design, CAD systems.

☐ determination of 'true' function, ie. what is the item/product actually for, what is its real purpose?

As stated above, value engineering is the concept of 'building-in' the VA concept during the pre-production process so that the product/process starts life having been value analysed. This does not preclude subsequent VA some years after launch of the product/process. During the intervening time, new processes and materials are likely to have become available and useful results may still be yielded from VA.

Chapter Summary

In this chapter the following areas relating to specifications have been considered:

☐ The importance of effective specifications, including considerations of what makes a specification effective and approaches to ensuring that specifications are effective.

☐ The types of specification commonly used, including their respective advantages and disadvantages.

☐ The team approach to specification development, including how any conflicting departmental views may be resolved.

☐ ESI and ECI and how both of these may contribute to better designs, the incorporation of best practice and the ultimate satisfaction or 'delight' of the end customer.

☐ VA and VE, the nature of these related concepts, what contribution they may make and the role of the procurement department in both of them.

Case Study

Doomray

Doomray Ltd is a medium sized manufacturing company producing electro-mechanical parts for the oil and gas industry. Its customers include all the major oil companies.

Recently, the company has decided to renew its fleet of fork-lift trucks (FLT) that are used to handle the various materials and components processed by the Company. In the past, the Company has renewed individual trucks as they have needed replacing. This has led to various types of FLT being used and has caused some problems, including spares and repairs. Now the Company has an opportunity to renew the whole fleet of 15 with a standard vehicle.

Bob Tuck, who is Head of Contracting, has been given the task of purchasing this new fleet. His first task is to establish a specification for the FLT. The materials handling engineer, James Rankin, has very strong views about the type of FLT they need, and has already had initial discussions with Yamomoto Industries, well-known manufacturers of FLT. The Head of Manufacturing, Jenny Springer, has made it clear that she will not tolerate anything less than the latest technology. She has also collected various technical details from a number of well-known manufacturers.

Bob has spent the last few weeks discussing the FLT problem with the various parties involved and a great deal of time writing up the technical specification of the FLT required. A local agent of Yamomoto, who has recently studied the specification, does not feel his company could produce such a vehicle without producing a "special" at great cost. Bob believes he will now have to go back to the drawing board. In the meantime, both Jenny and James are starting to negotiate with various suppliers about the supply of FLT, some of which are very expensive and seem to Bob to be totally in excess of their current and future needs.

Task

1. Evaluate the different needs of the stakeholders.

2. What has gone wrong with the process to date?

3. Create an Action Plan for the way forward, to reach a "Shared Vision".

3.   Quality Concepts and Practices

Introduction

Definition of Quality

'Quality is frequently defined as fitness, merit or excellence'.

Dobler & Burt (' Purchasing & Supply Management', 6th edition)

However, Dobler and Burt go on to state that 'quality has no meaning in procurement, except as it is related to function and ultimate cost'.

Before considering the specifics of quality, it would be useful to consider the general nature of product quality using the 'Eight Dimensions of Product Quality' (*Garvin*):

(overleaf)

Performance	The primary operating characteristics of a product, eg, sounds and picture clarity of television set.
Features	The additional functions or attributes of a product, eg, remote control unit for a television set.
Reliability	The chance that a product will fail within a specified time.
Conformance	The degree to which the product's design and operational characteristics match known standards.
Durability	The amount of use one gets from a product before it physically deteriorates i.e. its economic life.
Serviceability	The speed, ease, courtesy and competence of repair/maintenance.
Aesthetics	How a product looks, feels, sounds, tastes or smells.
Perceived quality	Products may be evaluated less on their objective characteristics than their images, advertising, reputation or brand name.

The following table shows two contrasting approaches to assuring quality.

Inputs	Competition and description	Process closed	AQL and inspection	Outputs
Inputs	ESI/Performance Specifcations See p 68	Process open	Zero defects	Outputs

Fitness for Purpose

It is interesting to note the contributions made by the quality experts to our overall understanding of the concept of quality. These are summarised in the table below.

Expert	Contribution
Deming	Ongoing process, check + act, SPC, prevention
Juran	Internal customers, role of suppliers and customers, brainstorming, total quality concepts
Feigenbaum	Total design quality concept, ESI, build-in quality, design issues
Ishikawa	Cause and effect, 4 M's methodology for analysis, quality circles
Crosby	'Quality is free' concept, price of non-conformance (PONC)

Many procurement people today use performance specifications. These tell suppliers not what the item to be supplied should look like or what its dimensions are. Instead, they inform the supplier as to what the item should be able to achieve. The item supplied may then be measured by the buyer's company in terms of whether it achieves its stated objectives. An example of this might be a pump that might have the following performance parameters or objectives:

☐ to have an overall size within certain dimensions.

☐ to have a limit as to its power consumption.

☐ to be able to pump a certain amount of fluid per minute or per hour.

The pump, when supplied, may then be measured in terms of whether it performs according to these parameters or, in other words, whether it is fit for the purpose specified.

It should be obvious that, in order to be able to use this form of measurement, the purpose of the item must be stated to the supplier at the outset.

Conformance to Requirements

This is an alternative form of specification and quality measurement to a performance specification. Here, the supplier is given precise details of what is required by the buyer's company often, although not always, in the form of an engineering drawing or blueprint. The supplier's job is then to produce the item in line with the specification.

The specification may then be used to measure the quality of the item supplied. The question that needs to be asked of the item, simply put, is 'Does the item conform to the specification or not?' For this reason, specifications used in this context are referred to as 'conformance specifications'.

It is worth commenting that, if a supplier is provided with a conformance specification and they supply exactly in line with the specification and the item does not perform as required, there is no legal redress against the supplier. On the other hand, with a performance specification, if the supplier assures the buyer that the item will perform as required and, in the event, it does not, the supplier can be held liable.

The Role of the Supplier

The role of the supplier in the achievement of quality is, at its simplest, to supply items in line with the quality levels required by the buyer. This is true whether the quality levels are indicated rigidly by means of a conformance specification or in a manner more open to interpretation by means of a performance specification.

Food for thought

Does your organisation prefer performance specifications or conformance ones? Does it have a preference of any kind?

Today, however, many buyers require their suppliers to be more proactive in terms of their involvement with quality issues. To this end, buyers will often encourage suppliers to suggest improvements to the items being supplied, and to become involved at the design stage of the item. This kind of involvement may take the form of encouraging the supplier to take part in design committee meetings. As we have seen, this process is known as 'early supplier involvement' (ESI). Alternatively, it might take the form of encouraging the supplier to make suggestions on an *ad hoc* basis whenever the supplier has an idea that he thinks might improve either the item supplied or the buyer's process.

In respect of the actual quality supplied much depends upon the supplier's commitment to quality. This may involve consideration of the following.

- Statistical Process Control, (SPC), uses statistical methods to prevent defects in production.

- Total Quality Management, (TQM), defined as 'a way of managing an organisation so that every job, every process, is carried out right, first time and every time'. – *C. K. Lysons ('Purchasing and Supply Chain Management' Prentice Hall).*

- Quality Control (QC) is a range of traditional methods such as inspection of items arriving from suppliers. This inspection may take place either at Goods Inwards or when the item is about to be used, depending on how easy it is to inspect just prior to use.

- Budget. Quality is often seen as being a function of cost. Is the item to be made down to a particular cost or up to a particular quality level? Much will depend, in this respect, on budgetary constraints.

- Culture and values. Is the buyer's company a 'high-quality' one or a 'low-budget' one – i.e. is it 'upmarket' or not? If it has a high-quality, 'upmarket' culture, buyers need to ensure that suppliers with a similar culture and set of values are selected.

- ISO 9000 sets out to measure a company's quality measurement procedures, and will provide guidance as to the selection of suppliers – usually stipulating what evaluation process a supplier needs to satisfy before becoming an approved supplier.

Food for thought

Does your organisation encourage suppliers to contribute to design or quality matters? What are the reasons for your answer?

Quality Assurance Tools and Techniques

Quality assurance may be defined as follows.

'All those planned and systematic actions necessary to provide adequate confidence that a product or service will satisfy given requirements for quality'.

There are a number of quality assurance tools, many of which are aimed not just at assuring a supplier's quality now, but at bringing about an improvement in quality over time. This idea of quality improvement is sometimes known by the Japanese name of 'kaizen', and is seen as being a major means of delighting the end customer. It includes the following features:

- clear fitness for purpose.

- certified suppliers.

- designed-in quality.

- quality processes.

- ESI + ECI.

- cost not price focus.

Specific techniques that may help in the processes of quality assurance and quality improvement are covered below.

Statistical Process Control (SPC)

Definition

'....statistical methods are employed to ensure that a quality capability is possessed by an organisation and that quality is maintained by a monitoring, feedback and adjustment system. The idea is that a proactive approach is taken to the prevention of defective material or service rather than the reactive 'correcting' approach of seeking to identify defective work already done'.

Baily, Farmer, Jessop and Jones ('Purchasing Principles and Management' Prentice Hall)

This is a quality control/assurance technique that is widely used in a number of industries. Its basic purposes are:

- to measure the dimensions of products coming off a machine.

☐   to identify whether there is a trend towards the dimensions going 'out of tolerance' (i.e. produced to dimensions that fall outside the engineering tolerances laid down – and, hence being 'scrap').

☐   in the event of such a trend being identified, to allow corrective action to be taken before items that are out of tolerance are produced so that no scrap is produced.

Failure mode and effects analysis (FMEA)

Definition

'A systematic approach that applies a tabular method to aid the thought process used by engineers to identify potential failure modes and their effects'.

C.K. Lysons ('Purchasing and Supply Chain Management' Prentice Hall)

This is a much more 'conceptual' approach to quality than the rather 'hands on' SPC. Briefly, it involves examining products, systems or any other aspect of an organisation deemed relevant (e.g. procurement and stores systems) with a view to identifying potential problems (i.e. things that may go wrong). Corrective action can then be taken in advance. If aspects that are highly likely to go wrong are corrected first; moving, by degrees, to aspects that are hardly likely to go wrong and correcting these should allow a 'fool-proof' system/product to emerge.

Food for thought

Is FMEA used in your organisation? If it is, what results are gained from its use? If not, what scope is there for its introduction?

Quality circles

Definition

'Quality circles are small groups of workers, usually numbering around six, whose role is to meet at regular intervals to discuss quality issues and ways of correcting quality problems'.

Many companies use quality circles to great effect with frequent reports of quality costs being reduced through their use.

An important aspect of quality circles is that they are composed of people at all levels of the organisation, including the shop floor. Because of this they are seen as being a way of allowing workers at all levels to be empowered (in this case to deal with quality issues).

This should allow workers to 'take ownership' of quality issues/problems as they relate to their own job and jobs around them.

This empowerment feeds into Total Quality Management (TQM) and the 'bottom up' approach to quality that TQM requires. Indeed, in many companies, quality circles are seen as being an essential tool for implementing TQM.

Quality circles fit into the rest of the organisation as shown in figure 1 below.

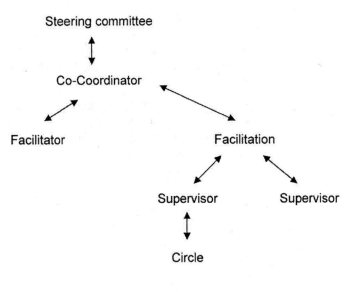

Figure 1

Quality control measures

Definition

'The operational techniques and activities that are used to fulfil requirements for quality.

> *C. K. Lysons ('Purchasing and Supply Chain Management' Prentice Hall)*

'Inspection activities…..along with other activities which involve monitoring to ensure that defectives (or potential defectives) are spotted'.

Baily, Farmer, Jessop and Jones ('Purchasing Principles and Management' Prentice Hall)

The term 'quality control' implies quality measures that take place after an item has been produced. The chief technique, here, is inspection. This is still widely used because, despite the increasing use of quality assurance techniques aimed at a zero defects outcome, many people believe that there is no substitute for inspecting items to ensure quality. Inspection may be carried out:

☐ at Goods Inwards at the buyer's premises.

☐ immediately prior to use at the buyer's premises.

☐ during, or, at the end of, the production process at the supplier's premises.

While inspection still has a part to play, many organisations are attempting to reduce its extent because of the view that quality cannot be 'inspected into' an item. All that inspection achieves is to identify problems that have already occurred and, as such, cannot contribute in any major way to zero defects or quality improvement. Additionally, inspection is time consuming and, therefore, costly.

Inspection may, however, help identify problems by being used on a 'sample' basis and may contribute in a major way to vendor rating schemes.

Costs of Quality

There are essentially three distinct costs associated with quality:

☐ costs of prevention.

☐ costs of identification of quality problems.

☐ costs of rectification of problems.

Food for thought

To what extent is inspection used in your organisation? How valuable does it appear to be? Is it being reduced in any way to make way for quality assurance techniques?

Traditional quality measures such as inspection, which seek to identify problems and allow their rectification, tend to have a high cost of identification and rectification. More modern approaches to quality management such as 'zero-defects' as well as SPC and FMEA, and proactive approaches to design such as ESI and ECI tend to have high cost of prevention but low costs of identification and rectification.

A move to more modern approaches might appear merely to be exchanging one set of costs for another. However, eminent writers on quality issues such as Philip B. Crosby and Genichi Taguchi have identified that the cost of 'getting it wrong' can be extremely high (as much as 40% of the value of a product according to Crosby). It follows, therefore, that focusing on getting quality right from the outset, i.e.'zero defects', is likely to reduce costs overall as well as avoiding such aspects as adverse publicity resulting from the need to rectify a serious problem.

These 'non-quality costs' may be illustrated as follows.

Process	Cost %
Manufacturer	1%
Rework	10%
Warranty claim	100%

Quality of Services

So far discussion of quality has focused on quality of products. Increasingly, however, organisations purchase services from outside contractors. The measurement of service quality is more difficult than the measurement of product quality, because of the intangible nature of services (they cannot be picked up and measured with a micrometer/ruler, etc.) This gives rise to the service quality gap, of which there can be more than one:

☐ in customer expectations.

☐ between the service quality specifications and what customers want.

☐ between actual service delivery and the specification.

☐ in external communications about the service between provider and customer.

☐ between the service customers expectations and their perception of the service they have received.

Perceptions of the quality of a service tend to be very subjective in nature. Here is a summary of the differences between materials and services and some of the problems associated with the procurement of services generally:

Differences	Problems
Intangible	Satisfaction
Local	Competition
Variable	Quality
Standard difficulty	Consistency/perception
Non-physical	Cost analysis
Legal issues	Perception
Contractor	Short term

Food for thought

What services are purchased in your organisation? How is quality measured? What difficulties, if any, are encountered when measuring them?

Total Quality Management (TQM)

Introduction

TQM is the concept of 'everybody, everything and every time'. Senior management play a vital role in the introduction and development of TQM, which can also can make a considerable contribution to the 'bottom line'.

TQM Concepts

TQM is at the forefront of quality thinking. However, rather than being merely an intellectual 'concept' it is a process, albeit conceptual in nature, that may deliver real benefits to organisations that are committed to its goals and that implement it in a cohesive, organised manner. TQM can be defined as:

'A philosophy that understands the relationship between inputs and outputs. It makes a vital linkage between all actions and events from input through process to final output in terms of quality'.

Carter and Price ('Integrated Materials Management', Pitman, 1993)

In terms of practical application of TQM, more is needed. Managers need to be able to break the overall concept down into manageable components that may be disseminated to staff and implemented by means of staff commitment. To this end, the following 'TQM approach' should be useful as it provides a framework for managers to grasp the essential nature of TQM.

A TQM approach

☐ A focus on the customer – one of the essential elements of TQM is that everything is focused on the customer, whether 'the customer' be external or internal. The concept of the internal customer is very important here. The idea is that, if everyone in the organisation treats the internal people with whom they have dealings as a 'customer', the level of quality and service provided to them will lead to a high level of quality and service being provided to the external customer.

☐ A commitment to total quality and investment in knowledge – without a genuine commitment to total quality by everyone, at all levels of the organisation, TQM will not work. Management need to foster this commitment in their staff and ensure that all steps are taken to gain as much knowledge as possible relevant to quality, its attainment and its improvement at all levels of the organisation.

☐ A foundation for continuous improvement – often known by its Japanese name of 'kaizen'. This is considered to be one of the main principles of TQM. Organisations should not take the view that whatever quality level they currently have will suffice for all time, but that improvement is always possible. Focusing on the ongoing improvement of quality levels is one method of achieving competitive advantage.

☐ A philosophy for running a business – early writers on TQM used to say that quality should become a corporate objective. If this happens, the focus of management and staff at all levels should be on quality and so the whole philosophy of the business becomes that of quality.

☐   A right way to manage – management of an organisation based on TQM principles will give many advantages: greater empowerment of staff and encouragement for staff to take ownership of quality matters/improvement, and competitive advantage to name but two. In this sense, TQM may be seen as much more than a quality measurement tool but rather as the 'right way to manage'.

☐   Total empowerment – one of the fundamental principles of TQM is that all staff, at all levels in the organisation, are 'empowered' so that they may take ownership of quality as it relates to their job. Staff are thus encouraged to devise ways of improving quality and reducing waste, to query any quality issues that arise from the performance of their job, and to solve any quality problems that may arise. In this way, motivation should be improved, as should the achievement of higher quality levels. Better motivated staff are more likely to be committed to the achievement of quality and its improvement.

Food for thought

Has TQM been introduced in your organisation? If so, has greater empowerment of staff been a fundamental part of it?

Everybody, Everything and Every Time

This introduces the '3 Es' of TQM, as established by Ray Carter of DPSS. These are fundamental principles of TQM and provide a useful framework around which to build a complete picture of what TQM is and how it works.

Total Quality Management

The 3 Es

☐   **Everybody** – all staff in the organisation from the chief executive down to the lowest levels such as cleaners, etc. should be made aware of the nature of TQM and its objectives. If everybody in the organisation performs their job to the highest possible level of quality and seeks to improve the quality of their job over time, the quality of product or service provided to the end customer will be enhanced and improved. It is considered important for the successful implementation of TQM that everybody 'signs up' to the ethos of TQM and is committed to it. 'Everybody' in this context should also be taken to include suppliers. An organisation cannot successfully implement TQM without its suppliers and supply chains, particularly the major ones, playing their part. The role of suppliers in this context is to embrace the TQM concept themselves, to develop an ethos of supplying zero defects and to improve quality over time. The role of the buyer here is to develop an awareness of TQM, its workings and its mutual benefits, with suppliers.

☐ **Everything** – TQM must concern all aspects of the business and should be an all-embracing concept. If aspects of the business are left out of the TQM 'loop' it is unlikely that the implementation of TQM will be entirely successful.

☐ **Every time** – there must be no occasions when things are allowed to slip through the net. TQM and its successful implementation demand that any quality problems are dealt with and that there should be no instances of allowing something to pass, this time, providing it is corrected in future. TQM and its successful implementation demand full attention to quality matters at all times.

In summary, TQM requires a completely new approach to the setting of quality standards, the measurement of quality and quality assurance. This approach may be contrasted with the 'old' approach by using the terms 'traditional' and 'new age', as follows.

Traditional approach

☐ AQL (acceptable quality level) – this presupposes that a certain level of defect is acceptable

☐ QA/inspection ownership – product is measured, usually by the person receiving the product, to identify any defects that may exist.

☐ Stockpile and remove defects – product is purchased in large quantities, a long time before use, to allow sufficient time and scope for inspection to identify defects and their subsequent rectification.

☐ Receipt audit and verification – quality control measures take place upon receipt of goods.

New Age approach

- ☐ Defect-free production is attainable and there is an assumption that this is possible.

- ☐ Self inspect. The responsibility for inspection is passed to the worker responsible for the job and introduces a certain amount of 'empowerment'.

- ☐ Rework at point of failure. This may be 'in-process' rather than at the end of everything.

- ☐ Vendor certification. Suppliers are certified based on rigorous evaluation or past experience, so that they have responsibility for ensuring the quality of their products.

Alternatively, the differences between the traditional and TQM approaches to quality may be contrasted as follows.

Traditional	Commercial
AQL	Zero defects
Inspection	Prevention
Quality control	Quality assurance
LSI (late supplier involvement)	ESI (early supplier involvement)
Price	Total cost
Quality via competition	Quality via co-operation

Food for thought

If your organisation has introduced TQM does it follow the '3Es' approach? If not, what elements are missing? If it does follow this approach are the benefits apparent?

The Role of Senior Management

The main role of senior management, in terms of TQM, is to introduce it to the organisation and ensure that everyone becomes committed to its ideals. There is a great deal of emphasis on the idea that TQM is a 'bottom-up' approach, which suggests that senior management has a limited role in its implementation.

However, the role of introducing TQM, 'cascading' its nature and benefits down the management hierarchy and monitoring its progress, are extremely important.

Additionally the backing of senior management is essential for the empowerment of staff, to make TQM work, as previously discussed. Quality circles are considered by many to be important tools for the implementation of TQM.

These issues may be discussed in more detail by considering the introduction of TQM.

- **Clear communication** – clear lines of communication operating both 'up' and 'down' the management hierarchy must be established. These will allow senior management to communicate any new initiatives that might feed into the TQM process and also allow feedback of such matters as operational difficulties in its implementation. There should also be two-way 'horizontal' communication between internal 'customers' and their 'suppliers'. In this way, ongoing difficulties relating to quality may be resolved and everyone will be able to work together towards the improvement of quality. It is the responsibility of senior managers to establish the need for this kind of communication and to set up systems to allow it to happen.

- **Culture change** – the culture of the organisation must be changed from whatever it is currently, for example one focused on output, to one where quality is everything. As has been mentioned previously under the '3 Es' approach, everyone must be focused, all the time, on quality. A change in an organisation's culture is usually driven by its stakeholders, the ones having the most 'hands on' influence being senior managers. This kind of organisational culture change, therefore, can only happen if initiated and completed by senior management.

- **Problem-solving groups** – at the start, the path of TQM will not necessarily be smooth, so it is useful for senior management to set up such groups to solve problems as they occur. In this way, any problems or difficulties that do occur will not cause the TQM process to grind to a halt.

- **Time** – it must be realised that TQM will not happen over night. Indeed, some writers on the subject take the view that it is never really achieved at all but has to be seen as an elusive ideal that managers work towards but that is always moving forward away from them. The term 'holy grail' has been used in this context to give the idea of something that, when approached, may be seen on the distant horizon but that, as one apparently comes closer, disappears or moves further away. This apparently mystical metaphor is useful because it gives the impression that TQM is never actually achieved or reached. While its purpose, in the light of such an idea, may be queried, it should be remembered that kaizen is an integral part of TQM. Part of the philosophy of kaizen is that there is always room for improvement, no matter how high a level of quality has already been achieved. Senior managers need to recognise this and accept that TQM will be a continuously evolving process.

☐ **Top-down and bottom-up** – TQM starts as a top-down process. Senior managers need to 'cascade' the benefits and methodology of TQM to lower levels in the management hierarchy. TQM is, thus, very much initiated by senior managers. However, once initiated, TQM should become a bottom-up process. Senior managers need to implement it in such a way as to allow everyone in the organisation to take ownership of quality, and to recognise their own responsibility to enhance and improve quality. Thus, once initiated and implemented in a top-down fashion, TQM should continue as a bottom-up process with quality initiatives originating from lower levels in the organisation.

☐ **Cross-functional approach** – senior managers need to recognise that, for TQM to be successful, it requires a high degree of cross-functional co-operation. The approach in some organisations whereby different departments communicate as little as possible with each other and only when they have to, is not conducive to the successful implementation of TQM. Senior managers need to take whatever steps are necessary to engender a culture of cross-functional co-operation so that quality matters may be identified and highlighted in a way that does not provoke recriminations. In this way, a culture of co-operation and 'working together' for a common purpose will develop and should have positive consequences for delighting the end customer.

As has been highlighted above, the process of TQM implementation is a gradual one and may be illustrated overleaf.

Progress to TQM

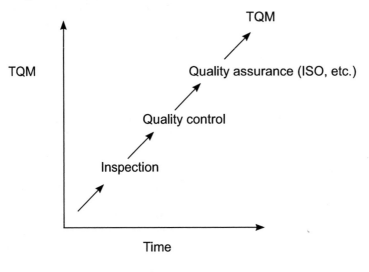

Figure 2

Contribution to the Bottom Line

At first sight it may seem as though TQM involves costs of implementation and, as such, will incur expense rather than contributing to the bottom line. However, if a long-term view is taken it can be seen that TQM will make a good contribution to the bottom line.

The nature of this contribution focuses on the concept of the costs of quality and may be summarised as follows.

☐   **Costs of quality are reduced** – this occurs despite the fact that costs of prevention will be increased. What should happen is that, because the costs of identification and rectification of problems will be significantly reduced, the overall cost of quality should decrease. Thus a direct contribution is made to the bottom line.

☐   **Enhanced company image** – a company that develops a reputation for high quality products or services through the use of TQM should gain competitive advantage and improve its sales. Thus, there is an indirect contribution to the bottom line that should be ongoing owing to the quality improvement element of TQM.

☐   **Reduced staff turnover** – the empowerment of staff that is an integral part of TQM should increase staff motivation and morale and lead to reduced turnover of staff. Apart from reducing the exodus of knowledge and skills that always occurs when staff leave the company, the costs of recruitment will be reduced, thus contributing, albeit perhaps in a small way, to the bottom line.

Chapter Summary

In this chapter some of the important aspects of quality assurance and quality control have been considered. These include:

☐ The distinction between the concepts of 'fitness for the purpose' and 'conformance to requirements' and the effect of this distinction on the use of specifications.

☐ The role of the supplier in achieving the right quality. This role is increasingly important given the increasing emphasis on outsourcing and the use of 'bought-out', as opposed to 'made in-house', items.

☐ Quality assurance techniques that may contribute to the increasingly important idea of quality improvement. Such techniques include SPC and FMEA.

☐ The role of quality control techniques such as inspection.

☐ The concept of costs of quality and how these may be reduced. In this section the concept of TQM has been covered, including:

- What TQM is and what benefits it may bring to an organisation

- How TQM should involve everyone in the organisation, everything touched by the organisation and how it should be at the forefront of everybody's mind every time.

- The crucial role of senior management in initiating and setting in motion the TQM process and in developing a 'bottom-up' approach that assists in engendering the 'everybody, everything, every time' approach referred to above.

- The contribution, both direct and indirect, that TQM may make to the bottom line.

4. The Tendering Process

Introduction

There are a number of critical stages in the tendering process from the identification of the need through to the award of the contract.

Definition

Firstly, it would be useful to define tendering:

> 'The procedure by which potential suppliers are invited to make a firm unequivocal offer of the price and terms which, on acceptance, shall be the basis of the subsequent contract'.

> *C.K. Lysons ('Purchasing and Supply Chain Management' Prentice Hall)*

There are two types of tendering.

    ☐   **Open tendering** – there is no restriction on the number of bidders allowed to submit tenders. Advertising the fact that tenders for a particular purchase are required should be as widely based as possible.

☐ **Selective tendering** – a preferred supplier list is used.

The Stages in the Tendering Process

There are a number of distinct stages between the original identification of the need to purchase something and the award of the subsequent contract. These may be illustrated by the flow diagram in figure 1 shown on p 47.

Food for thought

Does your organisation's tendering process follow the 'route' shown in Figure 1? If not, why not?

These stages will now be analysed in more depth, but it would be useful to consider the following.

Requirements for Effective Competitive Tendering

Many suppliers

Some buyers believe that three is enough. The actual number of proposals sought depends upon the nature of the goods or equipment to be purchased, how important they are to the buyer's organisation and how many vendors exist in the supply market. Generally, the requesting of bids from only three suppliers will not serve to 'stimulate the competitive pressures' that exist in the supply market to ensure that the buyer obtains the 'best' deal.

Clear specifications

If these are not clear (and unambiguous), it is likely that the suppliers, instead of requesting clarification, will 'pad' the price to cover unforeseen eventualities. The reason for this is fear of looking as if they are not experts in their field. If it happens, it undermines the whole purpose of competitive bidding.

Capable suppliers

There is no point in allowing suppliers who are not capable of providing the goods or service to submit proposals. This may occur because suppliers who are not experienced in the type of work required may indulge in 'kite flying'.

Suppliers who want the business

There may be many reasons why companies asked to submit a proposal might not want the business. It could be that the buyer's requirement falls outside the supplier's core business area, or that the buyer has a reputation for being difficult to deal with. If companies that are not interested in the business are asked to submit proposals, it not only wastes the buyer's time but also undermines the competitive bidding process.

Sufficient time

Sufficient time must be allowed for suppliers to prepare and submit proposals. Suppliers may have to ask their suppliers to submit proposals for raw materials, sub-assemblies, etc., all of which takes time. If suppliers are not given enough time for this, it is likely that they will simply 'pad' the price to cover unforeseen eventualities or they may miss something that might prove important later.

Value justifies the expense

The competitive bidding process is time consuming and requires much attention from the buyer. It is, therefore, an expensive process and should only be used when the expenditure under consideration is of sufficient value to justify the expense of the process.

It is worth commenting, at this point, that the question of bids versus a negotiated process comes up. Generally speaking, if any of the above-mentioned requirements for effective competitive tendering is missing for any reason, a contract should be awarded as a result of negotiation. This, too, can be an expensive process and its expense must be justified by its efficacy.

Competitive tendering and negotiation are not mutually exclusive, however. Both may be used in conjunction, via the process of post-tender negotiation, to develop satisfactory contracts and to build relationships with suppliers.

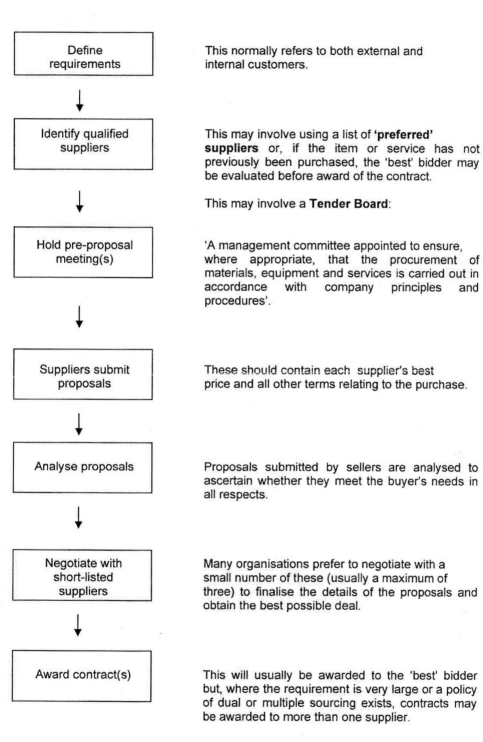

Define requirements	This normally refers to both external and internal customers.
↓	
Identify qualified suppliers	This may involve using a list of **'preferred' suppliers** or, if the item or service has not previously been purchased, the 'best' bidder may be evaluated before award of the contract. This may involve a **Tender Board**:
↓	
Hold pre-proposal meeting(s)	'A management committee appointed to ensure, where appropriate, that the procurement of materials, equipment and services is carried out in accordance with company principles and procedures'.
↓	
Suppliers submit proposals	These should contain each supplier's best price and all other terms relating to the purchase.
↓	
Analyse proposals	Proposals submitted by sellers are analysed to ascertain whether they meet the buyer's needs in all respects.
↓	
Negotiate with short-listed suppliers	Many organisations prefer to negotiate with a small number of these (usually a maximum of three) to finalise the details of the proposals and obtain the best possible deal.
↓	
Award contract(s)	This will usually be awarded to the 'best' bidder but, where the requirement is very large or a policy of dual or multiple sourcing exists, contracts may be awarded to more than one supplier.

Figure 1

Stages in the competitive bidding process

Define customer requirements

This is relatively easy if the 'customer' is internal; the buyer may work with the relevant departments to ensure that a specification that will be understood by the supply market can be drafted. The buyer should be able to contribute specific supply market information such as availability, standards, etc. If the item or equipment is required to satisfy an external customer, it is useful to obtain as much information from the customer about specific requirements, features, etc, so that these can be incorporated into the request for proposal.

Identify qualified suppliers

It is most important that qualified suppliers are identified, because requesting tenders from suppliers that are not qualified is a waste of time and resources and undermines the competitive bidding process in terms of its ability to help identify the 'best' supplier. The qualification comes about through a process of supplier evaluation.

In open tendering, where an advertisement is placed in the press/on the Internet, etc. to encourage would-be suppliers to come forward, the evaluation process will be carried out after likely suppliers have been identified by analysis of the tenders. In selective tendering, a pre-evaluation process is carried out to develop a list of approved suppliers and only companies on this list are requested to submit a tender.

Hold pre-proposal meeting(s)

It may be necessary to hold internal meetings with staff from all departments involved in the purchase, to ensure that requirements are identified and capable of being set down in the form of a request for proposal (RFP). This is done to ensure that requirements may be written down in the RFP in a way that is clear and unambiguous so that suppliers will have a clear understanding of the buyer's requirements.

When the purchase is a large piece of capital equipment or linked to a major project, it is common practice to hold pre-tender meetings. Here, suppliers or would-be suppliers are invited to a forum where they may ask questions and gain further information. The idea behind this is that all suppliers have access to the same information and may submit tenders 'on a level playing field'. This should assist the subsequent tender evaluation process. Following this, RFPs are sent out to would-be suppliers.

Suppliers submit proposals – these should be received by a stated time and it is useful if all suppliers submit tenders in the same format. This assists the evaluation/analysis process.

Analyse proposals – in many ways, this is fundamental to the tendering process. Proposals from suppliers are analysed to identify whose tenders may be discarded and likely suppliers from a shortlist may be developed. Many buyers subsequently carry out post-tender negotiation with short-listed suppliers.

It is useful to consider some common evaluation criteria for the tender process:

- understanding experience.

- organisational experience.

- these relate to the experience of the supplier in dealing with similar RFPs and products/ services.

- quality assurance mechanisms – e.g. whether they have ISO 9000 approval.

- appropriateness of organisational policies – whether the organisation is capable of working with the buyer's company and has a compatible culture.

- management information arrangements.

- innovation and creativity – whether the supplier is capable of being proactive in terms of product development or quality improvement.

- value for money – taking account of price, quality, service, etc.

- coverage - if our organisation hsa many sites, does the supplier have a wide enough 'spread' to service our requirements.

- appropriateness of methodology.

- experience and qualifications of staff/associates/subcontractors – it is particularly important to consider the capabilities of people, such as subcontractors, who will be doing much of the work if the contract is awarded, but who are not directly connected with the supplier, it is all too easy to allow them to slip through the evaluation 'net'.

- compliance checks.

In order to facilitate such analysis of tenders, it is common practice to use a bid analysis matrix to aid the analysis process and make the decision-making process clear. This might look something like the following, see figure 2:

Bid analysis

Criteria	Score (1-10)	Weighting	Score	Remarks
Quality	5	x2	10	
Time	8	x1	8	
Cost	5	x3	15	
Extra added values	3	x3	9	
Miscellaneous	2	x2	4	

Figure 2

Negotiate with short-listed suppliers

Many buyers carry out post-tender negotiation. The purpose of this is to discuss the tenders with those bidders on the shortlist to try to obtain better terms or to clarify aspects of the tender. The number of suppliers on such a shortlist varies but, commonly, includes the three 'best' suppliers. It is not uncommon to find that, after post-tender negotiation, the supplier that was in third place has become the preferred supplier.

Award contract(s)

The various terms discussed during the negotiation must be written into a legally binding contract. Contract terms will usually cover such aspects as:

☐ price/cost.

☐ delivery time(s).

☐ quality levels or service level agreement.

☐ after-sales service (for capital items).

☐ guarantee terms.

☐   installation and commissioning.

☐   payment terms.

This is a list of typical terms but the actual terms used will depend on the needs of the buyer's organisation and the nature of the item or service being purchased. As stated previously, in some circumstances it might be necessary to award contracts to more than one supplier. This is usually the case if the buyer's requirement is larger than one supplier could manage or if the buyer's company has a policy of dual or multiple sourcing.

Debriefing

It is common practice to debrief unsuccessful bidders after the contract has been awarded. There are two main benefits of this process.

'Establishing a reputation as a fair, honest, 'open' and ethical client.'

'Providing unsuccessful tenderers with some benefits for the time and money spent on preparing their tenders. This is likely to be of most value to smaller and newer suppliers. It will help all tenders to be more competitive in the future.'

C.K. Lysons – ('Purchasing and Supply Chain Management' Prentice Hall)

Debriefing topics

☐   **Cost** – Actual prices are confidential but it is considered acceptable to disclose a bidder's ranking in the tender list. Value for money (VFM) is more difficult. There is a view that it is not constructive to inform a bidder that they were lowest in cost terms but were not selected on VFM. The UK Government's Central Unit on Procurement states that '….the interviewee could, however, be told that although the price was competitive, other factors were more significant in the award decision'.

☐   **Schedules** – exceptionally long production and/or construction schedules.

☐   **Design** – deficiencies, higher operating costs.

☐   **Organisation/administration weaknesses.**

☐   **Experience** – where the experience of the tenderer is deemed to be inadequate for the demands of the contract.

- **Personnel** – where numbers, experience and quality of personnel, including management, are deemed inadequate.

- **Facilities/equipment** – outdated equipment or facilities.

- **Subcontracting** – too much reliance on subcontractors and inadequate control arrangements.

- **Cost and schedule control inadequacies.**

- **Industrial relations** – where the tenderer has an unsatisfactory record and no plans for improvement.

- **Quality management** – where control procedures relating to materials, methods, systems and people are deemed unsatisfactory.

- **Contract terms** – where these differ fundamentally from those of the client.

- **After-sales service** – inadequate arrangements for servicing to the supply of spares.

The extent to which suppliers/contractors need to be debriefed can depend upon both Risk and Value, as shown in the following matrix:

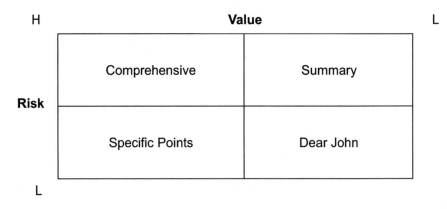

	Value	
H		L
	Comprehensive	Summary
Risk		
	Specific Points	Dear John
L		

Food for thought

Would you normally debrief unsuccessful bidders? If not, what are the reasons for not doing so? If you do debrief unsuccessful bidders, do you use the same criteria as above? What differences, if any, are there?

Other Aspects of Tendering

Tendering and total quality conflicts

The total quality concept suggests that the policies of single sourcing and 'partnership' be adopted so that the buyer may work with a chosen supplier over time to improve quality and develop a 'total quality' approach throughout the supply chain. Tendering may be perceived as being in conflict with this aim for the following reasons.

- Emphasis on price as a key variable – the total quality ideal suggests that total cost of ownership, of which quality is a major part, is more important than consideration of price alone.

- Long term quality degradation.

- Need for very tight specification – this goes against the total quality focus on performance specifications and commitment by the supplier to being proactive in terms of suggesting improvements to specifications and quality.

- Emphasis on lowest price – not lowest cost of supply.

- Lowest bidder is accepted so supplier base widens – the total quality approach tends to lead to a reduction of the supply base and an increase in the use of 'partnerships' with suppliers.

Note – Approved lists – it is a widely held opinion that the use of these can reduce or eliminate these areas of conflict. This is because the evaluation process leading to suppliers generally being included in the approved list, should focus on quality. Also, the development of an approved list means that the number of potential bidders is reduced, thus counteracting the tendency towards a widening supplier base.

When tendering is effective

Tendering is potentially a very expensive process. This expense may be justified by the savings and other benefits it may bring to the organisation.

The legal position of tenders

Whether an invitation to tender is an offer (see chapter 14) depends on the terms of the invitation. The tender will normally constitute an offer which, if accepted, forms the contract. If the invitation to tender implies that the potential buyer will require the goods, acceptance of a tender sent in response will result in a binding contract and the buyer will be obliged to buy the goods.

Disadvantages of tendering

- ☐   Contractors may quote a price that is too low leading to subsequent disputes if goods or services are unsatisfactory.

- ☐   Tendering is unsuitable for certain contracts. With plant contracts, consultation with one or more of the more favourable tenderers is often essential in order to clear up some technical points. These often result in the supplier making suggestions that will result in cheaper running and maintenance costs.

- ☐   The tendering process is too slow for emergencies.

- ☐   Where tenderers are accepted on the principle of the lowest price, credit may not be given to suppliers for past performance.

- ☐   Tendering can be an expensive procedure for the buyer.

- ☐   Tendering is expensive for the contractor.

Bid Analysis

Introduction

Bid analysis is an important procurement activity. It involves the comparison of quality, time and cost – QTC.

Definition of Bid Analysis

'The procedure by which potential suppliers are invited to make a firm unequivocal offer of the price and terms which, on acceptance, shall be the basis of the subsequent contract'.

Tools of Quotation Analysis

Firstly, it is useful to summarise these. Many buyers construct a document or spreadsheet showing the criteria used in comparing and analysing quotations, designed in such a way as to allow the buyer to add figures/comments against each criterion, showing how each potential supplier 'scores'.

This model is known as bid tabulation, and typically would contain the following criteria:

□   previous supplier history.

□   base price.

□   price for extras.

□   quoted delivery.

□   technical specifications and quality validity period – price fixing clauses, escalation formulas.

□   requested payment terms.

□   exchange rate clauses if of foreign origin.

□   carriage and insurance costs.

□   installation and/or training charges (if appropriate).

□   warranty period.

□   spares availability.

□   general and special terms and conditions of sale.

□   quantity required.

These criteria will now be considered in more detail.

Previous supplier history

A comment may be made on the bid tabulation document illustrating the kind of previous performance provided by the supplier, if there is any. Clearly, if the supplier is new to the buyer, no comment will be possible, but, if the selective tendering process is used, the supplier should have been thoroughly evaluated prior to the Request for Proposal (RFP) being sent. If the supplier has proved to be unreliable in the past, a comment to this effect may be made and may weigh heavily in the actual analysis process. This eventuality does beg the question, however, as to why an RFP was sent to such a supplier.

Base Price

This should include any cost breakdowns, discounts, price breaks, etc. Price is considered by many buyers to be the most important analysis criterion. It should be remembered, however, that there are many other criteria. Many buyers request that cost breakdowns accompany the quotation so that the buyer may see how the price is calculated and whether there are any price anomalies or queries. Examples of these might be where the supplier shows a raw material cost that is at variance with the buyer's information as to the true market cost of this material. Additions and subtractions such as discounts should always be considered so that, when comparing one supplier with another, comparison may be made on a 'like-for-like' basis. Price breaks (e.g. if the quantity purchased is 1-99, the item costs £20.00 each but, if 100-249 are purchased, the item costs £18.75 each) should be taken into account and compared. Price breaks may be important because, if they exist, by buying larger quantities less frequently, a better overall price may be achieved, assuming that this coincides with the buyer's overall requirements.

Price for extras

If some suppliers are offering a 'basic' product with the optional addition of extra features, and if such features are desirable from the buyer's viewpoint, their prices need to be added to the bid tabulation and analysed/compared.

Quoted delivery

It would be expected that most suppliers would quote against the delivery time requested by the buyer, in which case this ceases to be a criterion for quotation analysis, but some suppliers may have different ideas. It is important to be aware of any variances from supplier to supplier and to include these in the overall analysis/ comparison process. This is particularly true when repeat deliveries of items are required by the buyer, preferably at similar times each week/month, etc. It is also important when the buyer provides delivery 'windows' (e.g. delivery to take place between 10.00am and 11.00am, Friday 20th June) for suppliers and requires that deliveries be made during these windows without fail.

Technical specifications and quality

This criterion may be divided into two parts.

1. To what extent does the product offered match or exceed the specification - it would usually be expected that suppliers would offer quotations based on the specification provided by the buyer, thus leading to comparison/analysis of the quotations against other criteria. However, some suppliers might offer products of either higher or lower specification. It may be tempting to take the view that products of lower specification should automatically be ignored but it may be that they will suffice for the need and, at the same time, be cheaper or more readily available. In this instance, some analysis by technical staff may be necessary. Products of higher specification may perform better than originally anticipated but their ultimate cost, in terms of higher price/maintenance costs, etc. needs to be considered.

2. Quality standards, including use of recognised public standards - again, it would usually be expected that suppliers would offer quotations based on the quality levels stipulated by the buyer in the RFP. However, if one supplier produces items that satisfy a particular standard this should make their product stand out from those of other suppliers whose products do not satisfy the standard. Care should be taken because public standards often have fairly wide tolerance (e.g. +/- 10%) which, almost certainly, will not be acceptable for high-precision applications. The award of ISO 9000 series of standards and, increasingly, ISO 14000 series is internationally accepted and highly regarded. It should be remembered, however, that neither of these standards measures the actual quality of product. Their role is to monitor quality systems, the theory being that a supplier that has good systems will automatically produce a good product, but this does not necessarily follow. Also, when the great majority of companies have these awards it is difficult to use them to distinguish between suppliers.

Validity period

Price fixing clauses, escalation formulas – again, this 'composite' criterion is best divided into its constituent parts, as follows.

- **Validity period** – some suppliers may stipulate that their quotation is only valid for (e.g.) 30 days from the date of the quotation, whereas others may agree that it is valid for (e.g.) 12 months. If the quotation and its attendant analysis/comparison process are part of a wider project evaluation that, in total, is likely to take some time, care must be exercised. A price that is only valid for 30 days might be invalid by the time the buyer is ready to place an order with the supplier, thus rendering the quotation useless.

- **Price fixing clauses** – sometimes suppliers will agree to 'fix' their price(s) for a period of time after an order is placed (e.g. two years). On the surface, this appears useful because it would help the buyer with budgeting and the buyer's company with estimating its own selling price(s). However, care must be taken because the suppler will probably have 'factored' an estimate of inflation into the price which may be higher than any such estimate the buyer might make, thus rendering the price higher than it should be. Any such price fixing clause offered by a supplier may be used as part of the analysis/comparison process.

- **Escalation formulae** – these usually refer to long-term, high-value projects although they can be applied to lower-value items that are to be supplied regularly in large quantities. The purpose of such formulas is to provide a mechanism that is independent of, and therefore fair to both parties, for calculating the effects of specific, relevant inflation during the running time of the contract. The details of different formulas quoted by different suppliers may be used as a basis for quotation comparison because the different details may be more or less attractive to the buyer. Caution should be exercised if one supplier is offering a fixed price when all others want an escalation formula to apply to the contract because this supplier might be quoting a price that, while fixed, is very high.

Requested payment terms

Different suppliers may request different payment terms. For example, one supplier may request payment within 30 days of receipt of invoice by the buyer whereas another may request payment within 60 days. If the supplier requesting 60 days is selected, the payment term will allow the buyer's money to remain in the bank longer and earn interest, thus effectively giving the buyer an extra discount. This issue becomes more complex when progress payments are required for a contract of long duration (e.g. a construction contract). Progress payments are used to assist the supplier to fund large, expensive contracts and involve the buyer paying in agreed percentages of the contract price at agreed stages of completion of the contract. Any supplier requesting 'cash with order' is likely to disadvantage the buyer, because any such payment will adversely affect the buyer's company's cash flow. It should be remembered that many more companies go into liquidation owing to cash flow problems than to lack of profitability.

Exchange rate clauses and duty if of foreign origin

These must be added to the supplier's quoted price, where applicable, and be included as part of the analysis/comparison process. Generally, exchange rates fluctuate daily (by small amounts) and at times of volatility on the currency markets they can be very difficult to forecast with any accuracy. However, relative exchange rate differences between the buyer's currency and other currencies can have the effect of making similarly priced items very different in terms of net price. Duty, payable on goods imported into the buyer's country from other countries, varies depending on both the country of origin and the nature of the goods. However, duty payable on an imported item can have the effect of making a reasonably priced item, from a country on whose goods a high rate is payable, more expensive than a higher priced item from a lower-duty country of origin.

Carriage and insurance costs

If they are quoted separately they must be added to the supplier's price and used for analysis/comparison purposes. If tenders from overseas suppliers have been received they may contain reference to INCOTERMS, and the stipulations of the specific term used must be studied carefully. Where there are differences between vendors who use different terms, comparisons should be made. As an example, a supplier submitting a proposal based on the EXW (Ex-Works) INCOTERM will require the buyer to collect the goods at the supplier's premises and pay for their transportation /insurance/packaging, etc. for the entire journey to the buyer's premises. Such a supplier may appear to be submitting a favourable price but, on investigation, may be more expensive than a supplier submitting a quotation based on the DDP (Delivered Duty Paid) INCOTERM, even though this latter's price may, on the surface, appear more expensive.

Installation and/or training charges

These both generally refer to pieces of capital equipment. If the buyer wants to acquire a piece of new machinery it will usually have to be installed and the supplier may offer to perform this task. A separate charge may be quoted for this work and will have to be included in the analysis/comparison process. The buyer may be tempted to look elsewhere for a contractor to perform this work, but caution needs to be exercised because the original supplier will usually be an 'expert' at this kind of task. Some of the buyer's company's workforce may need to be trained to use new equipment in order to get the best use out of it and any such training charges quoted by different suppliers may be included in the comparison process. Caution should be exercised over suppliers offering such services 'free of charge'. These charges will almost certainly have been 'factored' into the purchase price of the item.

Warranty period

This refers to pieces of capital equipment where it is normal for buyers to negotiate meaningful, working warranties with suppliers. The duration of any such warranty, offered by one supplier, may be longer than that offered by other suppliers and its terms may be more beneficial. All other criteria being equal, it would be better to purchase from the supplier offering the better warranty.

Spares availability

This applies particularly to unique pieces of capital equipment made especially for the buyer's company ('bespoke' items). 'Off-the-shelf' items do not normally present a problem in this respect because spares are usually readily available and will continue to be so for the foreseeable future. However, for 'bespoke items', the longer the supplier is willing to make spares available, the longer the buyer's company may expect to enjoy service from the equipment. There is little point investing a large amount of money in a piece of capital equipment if it has to be scrapped in three years' time for the want of a minor spare part. Different spares availability periods offered by different suppliers may be used as a point of comparison of tenders.

General and special terms and conditions of sale

There is often a conflict between the buyer's terms and conditions of contract and those of the supplier. This fact may apply both to general terms and any special terms that a supplier may wish to apply to a particular contract. As a general rule, the buyer should try to make all contracts subject to his/her own terms but this may not always be possible. All tenders should be searched thoroughly for any real problem terms so that these may be negotiated with the supplier, as necessary. A supplier who has fewer terms that are at variance with those of the buyer will, with other criteria being equal, be in a better position to be awarded the contract.

Quantity

Normally suppliers will quote against the quantity or quantities requested by the buyer and no question arises. Some suppliers, however, may quote for something different, e.g. if the buyer has requested 200 of an item to be delivered every month, a supplier may offer 300 delivered every 6 weeks to reduce delivery costs. Alternatively, if the buyer has requested a quotation for 750 of an item, a supplier may submit a quotation based on their minimum order quantity of 1000. In instances such as these, the buyer would need to examine the situation carefully and ascertain whether his/her company could accept such a change to the requested delivery and whether any benefit would derive from it. Particular care needs to be taken with quotations for 'rolling' quantities to be delivered each week, each month, etc.

Whether the supplier is offering direct ordering or call-off facility

This refers, in the main, to such items as consumables or 'maintenance repair' and operational (MRO) items. Here the buyer may wish to 'call-off' these items on a regular basis or set up a system whereby the user department requests them directly from the supplier in a bid to reduce paperwork and time. In this instance, if one supplier were able to offer such a service, it would be major point of comparison between suppliers.

Food for thought

Does the above list of tender analysis criteria agree with the list used in your organisation? If not, what differences are there? Are there any other criteria used?

The Role of the Customer

Sometimes, items are to be purchased against specific customer orders and, in such situations, the customer may wish to play a part in the evaluation of quotations from potential suppliers. In this instance, the buyer will need to collaborate with the customer's representatives in evaluating quotations. Such customer collaboration may be purely advisory, with the decision as to contract award being left to the buyer, or the customer may insist on having the final say. Customer input may be sought in a direct manner, as outlined above, or in a more indirect manner such as via early customer involvement or simultaneous engineering. This latter involves incorporating the views of all interested parties, including the customer, at the design stage.

Conferences involving both suppliers and customers have been known to take place with positive effect for all parties as the following case study illustrates.

'...A defence contractor was striving to react to the shrinking military market brought about by the 'peace dividend' at the start of the 1990s by diversifying into new sectors of business. Working with new suppliers and new customers at the same time meant that the learning cycle had to be done in parallel. What better way than to tackle it simultaneously? As a strategically important bid approached, the opportunity was seized to engage the help of key potential suppliers in some of the discussions with the potential customer.

This three-tier cross fertilisation of ideas stimulated shared problem solving on the difficulties of the proposed specification and prompted valuable cost and time saving suggestions, which may otherwise never have appeared. It certainly seemed to work since, rather against the odds, the defence contractor won the business and a real opportunity to become established in an exciting and expanding market.'

Chadwick and Rajagopal – ('Strategic Supply Management', Butterworth Heinemann)

Comparisons of Quality, Time and Cost

The buyer needs to compare and contrast these somewhat different variables with respect to suppliers' quotations. This process can be difficult because of the very different nature of each of them. Questions need to be asked, by the buyer, with respect to the quotations.

☐ Is the extra level of quality worth the extra price?

☐ Does the supplier with the lowest cost give the buyer the level of service required?

☐ Do the price, quality and service add up to the best value?

The buyer needs to identify not just the supplier with the lowest total cost but the one that can demonstrate:

☐ technical competence.

☐ strong managerial ability.

☐ a good track record.

☐ overall value for money against selection criteria.

Problems Associated with Tender Evaluation

☐ Insufficient criteria to enable a fair comparison to be made.

☐ Lack of experienced staff to evaluate the tenders properly – the importance of experience and training in this respect cannot be overstated.

☐ Spotting strategic tendering – suppliers who are not really interested in the business but who just want to find out market intelligence or information about the buyer's organisation.

☐ Encouraging competitive bids – sometimes suppliers are surprisingly reticent to submit quotations. There may be many reasons for this, including lack of capacity, or that what they are being asked for does not quite fit into their product portfolio, or that the buyer's company has a reputation for creating problems or for late payment of invoices.

☐ The work needed to document all the decisions.

☐ The need to have all the relevant information available.

Chapter Summary

In this section the important procurement activity of tender evaluation has been considered. This has involved examination of:

☐ the basic methods of tender evaluation, including the main criteria for reaching a suitable conclusion.

☐ the need to evaluate and compare/contrast often disparate and source selection criteria.

☐ problems that may be associated with tender evaluation.

Case Study

On the Carpet

The Department of Rural Affairs has a policy of maintaining staff facilities at a reasonable level of comfort wherever possible. Julie Summers is the Contracts manager and reports directly to the director of the Board. Part of Ms Summers' responsibilities is to purchase the fixtures and fittings needed for the staff canteen, and rest room area (See Fig 1) in the main office building. This area also acts as the company's social club at weekends.

Recently, Ms Summers was called upon by the Director to source a supply of good quality carpet for the canteen area. The budget set for this purchase was £7000 including supply, delivery and fitting costs. It would be a great advantage if the same budget could also be stretched to carpet the rest room. The specification for the carpet (established by the General Maintenance Department) is Grade II Axminster.

Ms Summers decided to seek bids from three suppliers. She has dealt with each of these companies in the past and has been equally satisfied with their performances. Within a few days the suppliers responded with three formal quotations (See Appendices 1, 2, and 3).

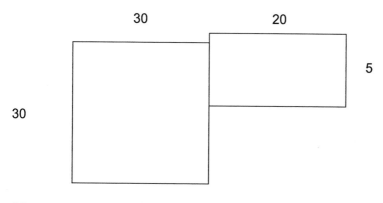

All measurements are in yards

Figure 1

Appendix I

Chiltern Flooring Contracts
Lightwater Trading Estate
Amersham, Bucks

Dear Sirs,

Thank you for your enquiry for Grade 11 Axminster carpet. We are pleased to quote as follows:

Price

£6.25 per square yard for quantities up to 1000 square yards; £6.00 per square yard for quantities of over 1000 square yards. Fitting charges are excluded (see below).

Delivery

We hold considerable stocks of the above carpet and would expect to make delivery within four weeks of receipt of order. The above prices do not include delivery charges which would be additional based upon the distance from our warehouse and the number of delivery points

Terms

We would request prompt payment of our invoice, and in this respect can offer a 2.25 per cent discount for payments received within 30 days of invoice.

Fitting

Our fitting charges are based on the total area of carpet and the length of the boundary edge as follows:

Area £1.00 per square yard
Boundary £3.00 per linear yard

Carpet Tiles

Whilst you have not requested a quotation for carpet tiles, may we take this opportunity of pointing out that at the present time we hold considerable stocks of carpet tiles which can be offered at the special price of £5.45 per square yard, ex stock, subject to remaining unsold. No fitting service is available for carpet tiles.

J Smith
Sales Manager

Appendlx 2

Alsford Carpets Ltd
Alsford
Worcs

Dear Sirs,

Re your enquiry ref 811 dated 30 March for Grade II Axminster carpet, we quote as detailed below:

Price

Supply of Axminster Carpet	£6.00 per square yard
Delivery charges per journey to one location	£100.00
Additional delivery points on the same journey are subject to an additional charge of £10.00.	
Fitting charges	£2.00 per square yard
plus £1.00 per perimeter yard	

The above prices are fixed for the next six months.

Delivery

Delivery and fitting can be completed in one month from receipt of order.

Terms of payment

Nett cash monthly. We regret that no settlement discount can be given on this order.

B Wright
Sales Manager

Appendix 3

Brevington's
New Mills
Derbyshire

Dear Sirs,

Grade III Axminster carpet

We are in receipt of your enquiry for the above mentioned goods and are pleased to quote as follows:

Price

Our prices inclusive of delivery and fitting charges are as follows:

Up to 800 square metres	£9.95 per square metre
Over 800 to 1600 square metres	£9.50 per square metre
Over 1600 square metres	£9.30 per square metre

These prices are subject to confirmation on receipt of your official order.

Delivery

At the present time we are able to quote a delivery of two weeks from receipt of order. This is subject to change and can only be confirmed on receipt of your official order.

Fitting

Our fitting service charges are included in the prices quoted above. Fitting will take between two and three days and can commence as soon as delivery is made. If however, you are not in a position to allow fitting to commence immediately upon delivery, we reserve the right to make additional charges to cover any extra costs we may incur.

Terms of payment

Nett cash monthly. We reserve the right to make an additional charge of 1.75 per rent per month on balances outstanding after one month. You will appreciate that this is necessary to enable us to continue to offer the most favourable prices to our customers.

Yours faithfully
R J Brown

Task

Critically evaluate the bids provided by these contractors and how would you deal with the issue of the carpet tiles?

5. Supplier Selection and Evaluation

Introduction

The critical criteria for the selection of the 'right' supplier will include consideration of the well-known DPSS 9 C's model for supplier selection, the importance of having an effective selection process, weighting systems, validity and evidence.

Definition of Supplier Appraisal

'Pre-order evaluation of a supplier to check that they have the capability, capacity, commitment and financials to process the order to meet your requirements.'

Many writers on procurement state that supplier selection is one of the most important aspects of the buyer's job. Great care must be taken over the manner in which supplier selection and appraisal are carried out.

Critical Selection Criteria

DPSS provides a useful model to help analyse selection criteria. This is the 9 C's model.

The extent and rigour with which this well-known process is applied is dependent upon a number of factors, including:

- □ risk.

- □ spend.

- □ criticality.

- □ complexity.

Supplier Contractor Evaluation – 10 C's

1. Competency.

2. Capacity.

3. Consistency.

4. Control of process.

5. Cost/price.

6. Commitment to quality.

7. Clean.

8. Culture and relationships.

9. Cash/finance.

It may be useful to set these criteria out in a matrix format so that the supplier's rating against the criteria may easily be examined, as below.

	C1	C2	C3	C4	C5	C6	C7	C8	C9
1									
2									
3									
Totals									

A typical supplier appraisal process might be as follows:

     ☐   define Critical Criteria (Cs).

     ☐   differentiate between 1-5 via key statements. These can be generally defined as: negligible, discernible impact, disruption of normal operations, significant impact and highly detrimental to core business.

     ☐   collect data.

     ☐   classify suppliers.

Competency

'Able to do'

Evidence – evidence of a supplier's capability is always required. Suppliers will always claim that they have an unimpeachable track record, but these claims should always be viewed with some scepticism unless supported by evidence. Such evidence may take the following forms.

     ☐   **Training and development** – what evidence exists that the supplier has a planned system for the training and development of staff, particularly regarding key initiatives that may help the supplier become 'world class'?

     ☐   **CVs/Qualifications** – CVs and records of the qualifications of all key staff should be available for inspection. The presence of highly qualified staff is no guarantee of a company's performance but it is a guide.

     ☐   **Key people** – who are they? They should be identified and interviewed, where possible, to ascertain their role in the supplier's performance and in the supplier's ability to perform to a high level in future.

     ☐   **Recruitment** – what records exist of the supplier having recruited people into key positions and the criteria applied to the recruitment of those people?

Capacity

'To meet present and future demands'

Evidence

     ☐   **Order book** – what is the state of the supplier's order book?

Unfortunately, the answer to this question requires some interpretation. If the supplier's order book is full, it means, on the one hand, that many customers have faith in the supplier and have awarded many contracts to them. This is a good 'pointer' to the supplier being a good one. On the other hand, a full order book may mean that the supplier, realistically, will be unable to do justice to the buyer's order, should one be placed, and provide the required service.

☐ **Operational statistics** – does the supplier have statistics providing evidence of such issues as quality problems or service level expressed as a percentage? If the supplier is ISO 9000 accredited, some evidence should exist. Good suppliers that are not accredited should be able to provide evidence of their past performance. It should be remembered that, just because a supplier has been 'good' to other customers in the past, there is no guarantee that they will be equally good in future.

☐ **Plant capacity** – what is the total capacity of the supplier's plant? If a contract is awarded to them and they prove to be a good supplier, do they have sufficient capacity to enable them to accept more work in future?

☐ **Forecasts** – what future business does the supplier forecast that it is likely to obtain? If a large amount, it is a good sign of confidence, but how and where will the supplier be able to fit in the buyer's business in this event?

☐ **Administrative resources** – Does the supplier have the necessary systems and procedures to support good quality and service? An example is an efficient sales order processing system so that the buyer may be confident that orders will be processed efficiently and effectively. Another would be an efficient production control system so that, once the order has been processed, the buyer knows that it will be possible to track its progress through the supplier's production process. A good expediting system may be linked to this to enable buyers' queries regarding the progress of their orders to be dealt with smoothly and efficiently.

☐ **Site visit** – for many buyers this is the most valuable tool in their possession in terms of evaluating potential suppliers. A site visit can tell the buyer much about how the supplier conducts his business in general, as well as about his capacity in particular. For example, claims that a supplier may make about having capacity all used up are difficult to support if it is obvious that the supplier's premises are virtually empty of raw material with few obvious signs of work taking place. A site visit is a good opportunity for the buyer to challenge the supplier as to aspects of quotations that are not clear or that do not appear to make sense. Site visits are also useful, in a general sense, for buyers, because they allow the buyer to learn about industrial processes - information which adds to the buyer's general experience/ knowledge.

Consistency

'Able to provide consistent levels of quality and services'

Evidence

☐ **Reputation** – what is the supplier's reputation? This may be gauged from a variety of sources such as knowledge gained from (e.g.) newspaper articles about the supplier and casual conversations with other members of staff. The buyer's experience and the supply market knowledge that comes with it cannot be overstated here. The buyer should have a 'feel' for the quality of a supplier gained from supply market knowledge, although it should be remembered that a good reputation is no guarantee of good quality or service.

☐ **Outputs** – it may be useful for the buyer to request that his/her Quality manager inspect a sample of the supplier's output to ascertain product quality at first hand.

☐ **History** – it is useful for the buyer to request references relating to other customers from the supplier. These should be followed up so that the buyer may gain a picture of the kind of quality and service that the supplier is providing to other customers. Is it consistent? What problems, if any, are regularly encountered. While this may be a useful process, it should be remembered that good supplier performance in the past is no guarantee of good performance in the future.

Food for thought

Think about situations where you have purchased from a supplier that had a good reputation. When you started placing orders with the supplier, were the service and quality actually received the same as those that the supplier's reputation suggested?

Control of Key Processes

- ☐ Inventory.

- ☐ Quality.

- ☐ Operations.

- ☐ Procurement.

- ☐ Marketing.

- ☐ Distribution.

- ☐ HSE (Health and Safety and the Environment).

It is important to try to gain a 'feel' for how the supplier manages and controls these 'key' processes. Each is important, in its own way, in terms of ensuring that the supplier is able to supply the goods, at the right time, of the right quality, at the right price, delivered to the right place, in the right quantity (the 5 'rights' of procurement). There follow examples of how each of these might contribute to the achievement of the '5 rights'.

- ☐ **Inventory** – if the supplier carries enough stock he is likely to be able to supply the right quantity at the right time. On the other hand, carrying too much stock will adversely affect the supplier's ability to supply at the right price because of excessive input costs.

- ☐ **Quality** – control of the supplier's quality processes enables the supplier to supply at the right quality. Conversely, over-specification of quality requirements may adversely affect the supplier's ability to supply at the right price.

- ☐ **Operations** – good control of operations will enable the supplier to supply at the right time and in the right quantity and will have an effect on the right quality.

- ☐ **Procurement** – efficient procurement, utilising the latest sourcing 'tools', will affect all the '5 rights', because companies are heavily dependent on key suppliers to provide good quality, service, innovation, etc., while keeping costs down.

- ☐ **Marketing** and to a greater extent, **distribution** – good, efficient processes here will allow the supplier to supply at the right time and in the right quantity.

☐ **HSE** – good systems and procedures here, such as a good safety record will contribute to the morale and motivation of the supplier's workforce. A well-motivated workforce will affect all of the '5 rights'.

Inefficiencies in any of these areas can cause the supplier's costs to escalate. Many buyers take the view that knowledge of suppliers' costs will allow the buyer to identify inefficiencies and make suggestions to the supplier as to how such inefficiencies may be eradicated, to mutual benefit.

Cost

Full cost analysis – full cost breakdowns should be obtained from the supplier and a full analysis carried out to examine the following.

☐ **Profit** – is the supplier profitable? If the supplier is not making sufficient profit then it is unlikely that they will remain in business in the medium to long term. It is, therefore, in the buyer's interests to ensure that suppliers remain profitable. There is an old-fashioned view favoured by some buyers that a supplier's profitability is no concern of the buyer's. However, it should be remembered that, if a supplier goes into liquidation, in the short-term the buyer will be without supplies and, in the long-term, will have to go through the entire sourcing process again at great use of time, effort and cost.

☐ **Variable costs** – costs directly associated with production and which increase with production volume. Usually, they are direct labour costs and direct material costs. Questions that may arise are include: is the supplier paying the workers the 'going rate' for the work and is the supplier paying the right price for raw materials and components? If the supplier is paying high wages to workers, input costs will be too high, but paying less than the 'going rate' may result in industrial unrest and supply delays. Similarly, paying too much for materials will result in input costs being inflated and a high selling price, whereas paying too little may have adverse quality effects.

☐ **Fixed costs** – The buyer should assess and analyse the specific level of such contribution. The costs associated with such things as indirect labour (labour or staff not directly concerned with output), energy, rent etc. It is usual for the selling price of a product or service to contribute to these fixed costs. The buyer should assess and analyse the extent of this contribution. Over contribution from the selling price means that the selling price is too high, whereas under contribution means that the supplier is in danger of going into liquidation.

☐ **Margins** – what is the supplier's profit margin? It should be remembered that all companies (including suppliers) must make a profit. If not, they will not survive for very long and, in the event of their going bankrupt, the buyer would be without a supplier. This is not a desirable state of affairs. The question is: what profit margin should a supplier make?

Food for thought

What would you regard as a fair profit margin for a supplier? Why?

☐ **Break-even point** – this is the quantity of production where total costs equal revenue. Above this point the supplier makes a profit and below this, a supplier will make a loss. It is useful for the buyer to be aware of the supplier's break-even point because it may have a bearing on the supplier's optimum production quantity. One way to ensure that the buyer is paying the right price is, if possible, to buy the supplier's optimum production quantity.

Commitment to Quality

Does the supplier have a quality policy and a commitment to its success? This may be assessed by examination of whether the supplier used any or all of the following.

☐ **SPC – Statistical Process Control**. A statistical method for measuring the actual quality of product and for identifying trends to slip outside tolerance limits and taking corrective action before a problem actually occurs. This helps to enhance quality and, at the same time, keep costs associated with quality down.

☐ **TQM – Total Quality Management**. A quality-conscious attitude throughout the organisation that should help guarantee improved quality to the end customer.

☐ **QC – Quality Control**. What specific measures does the supplier employ to measure the quality of output?

☐ **CIP – Constant Improvement Processes**.

☐ **Culture and values** – does the supplier have an organisational culture and a set of corporate values, communicated to everyone who works there, which focus on quality and its achievement/

improvement at all times? Some management thinkers/writers state that organisational culture is one of the most important aspects of a company in terms of its ability to be effective and successful.

☐ **ISO 9000** – is the supplier accredited to this standard? Accreditation of a supplier to such a standard is no guarantee of quality but should be a good guide and should guarantee a sound quality system. Other possible standards that assess quality are QS 9000 (American car manufacturers' more stringent version of ISO 9000) and ISO 14000 (this includes an environmental standard).

Clean

Suppliers and products should satisfy legislative and other environmental requirements.

Culture and Relationships

Suppliers and purchasers should share similar values. The importance of organisational culture has been considered earlier in this chapter. There is increasing importance given to the nature of the relationship that is likely to exist between the buyer and the supplier (organisational). Some buyers try to assess this relationship on an ongoing basis.

Cash/Finance

'Financial Stability'

Evidence

☐ **Balance sheet** – a record of fixed and current assets and how they have been financed.

☐ **Profit and loss account** – This is an account of the supplier's trading over the previous year. It indicates the difference between the company's income and the costs of running the business and indicates whether the supplier is making a profit or not.

☐ **Credit rating** – a rating by financial institutions, such as banks, of how credit worthy the supplier is. A poor rating should sound a warning and should be investigated.

☐ **Reputation** – what kind of reputation for, e.g. financial propriety or profitability, does the supplier have? This kind of information may be found out via the 'grapevine'.

The following financial analysis ratio provides a useful model for assessing a supplier's financial performance.

$$\text{Rate on assets} = \frac{\text{Profit x 100}}{\text{Assets}} \times 100$$

$$\text{Current ratio} = \frac{\text{Current assets}}{\text{Current liabilities}}$$

$$\text{Liquidity ratio} = \frac{\text{Current assets minus inventory}}{\text{Current liabilities}}$$

$$\text{Debtors Turnover} = \frac{\text{Debtors}}{\text{Turnover}} \times 52$$

Continuous Vendor Assessment

The supplier selection and evaluation process should not be a once-only process. When a supplier has been approved and has been awarded contracts some form of performance monitoring should be carried out on an ongoing basis to ensure that the supplier continues to perform in a satisfactory manner. This monitoring or assessment process should include the following variables:

☐ relationship

☐ culture

☐ Q.T.C. factors

☐ service/response

☐ trust factor

☐ adding value.

The process should not include a one-way blame attachment process, often used in a shallow manner by purchasers, to de-select suppliers and to chastise others with whom they wish to continue business.

Food for thought

Does your organisation have a formal supplier selection and evaluation process? If so, is it similar to that outlined above? If not, what differences are there?

Weighting Systems

The process of supplier evaluation and selection considered above involves the assessment of a number of different criteria concerned with the supplier's performance. These criteria will have different levels of importance from one buyer to the next and, for the same buyer, from one purchase to the next. To attempt to allow for these different levels of importance, it is usual to allocate a statistical weighting to reflect the importance attached to each criterion, ie. to the variables used to assess suppliers. If all criteria are considered by the buyer to be of equal importance there is no need to apply a weighting model or, alternatively, all criteria may be weighted equally.

The following table illustrates the working of such a system:

Criteria	Weight	Supplier A Score		Supplier B Score		Supplier C Score	
		Raw	Weighted	Raw	Weighted	Raw	Weighted
Quality	4	8	32	9	36	4	16
Delivery	3	10	30	6	18	10	30
Paperwork	2	10	20	10	20	10	20
Price	1	6	5	10	10	10	10
Totals		34	88	35	84	34	76

The Importance of Validity and Evidence

It is important that supplier selection and evaluation be carried out in as objective a manner as possible, although, inevitably, there will be elements of subjectivity. To make the evaluation system as objective as possible it is important that all criteria applied to the process are valid in terms of measuring aspects of a supplier's performance that are relevant to the purchase being considered.

Also, it is important that evidence to support views and assumptions made about the supplier is gathered. Without such evidence, views and assumptions are just that. With evidence they take on a much more factual aspect. To this end, it is important to collect as much data as possible relative to the particular supplier being evaluated/ assessed.

It should be remembered that there are two major drawbacks to this process of data collection.

    ☐   the high cost of collecting data.

    ☐   supplier performance is often affected by circumstances over which the supplier has no control.

Chapter Summary

In this chapter we have considered the important process of supplier selection and evaluation, including:

    ☐   consideration of the main criteria for supplier evaluation including the 9 C's model.

    ☐   the need to follow up the evaluation/assessment process with some kind of ongoing performance assessment.

    ☐   the need to apply some form of weighting to the assessment process to ensure that any calculations are as meaningful as possible.

    ☐   the importance of criteria adopted for supplier evaluation/ assessment being valid and the need to collect data by way of evidence to support any assumptions made.

Case Study

Dublin Corporation

After many successful years in the electrical contracting field, the Dublin Corporation decided to go into the business of manufacturing and installing air diffusers in commercial and industrial buildings. The move was logical in view of the Company's long experience in the fabrication and installation of electrical systems. Purchasing could be handled by an expansion of the present buying department, which already had considerable experience with many components similar to those used in the ventilation system - sheet metal, ducting, fasteners and so forth. John Berlin, who had been Dublin's purchasing agent, was named Director of Purchasing and given responsibility for getting the new division's purchasing program under way immediately.

Dublin Corporation's shop force was also expanded to handle assembly and installation of the diffusers. Several experienced machine operators and an additional foreman were added, all under the supervision of Bill Anderson, works manager.

Because of the early establishment in the industrial area in which it was operated, the high quality of its work, and its record of on-time performance Dublin Corporation had had little effective competition in the electrical field. As a result, the Purchasing Department, although not indifferent to price, had concentrated on quality and assurance of prompt delivery in dealing with suppliers. Prospects for competition in the air distribution field were different, however, both from equipment manufacturers and from contractors already well established.

Berlin took personal charge of establishing new supply sources for major items that the company had not previously bought. The most important of these were the production stampings used in the diffusion unit placed in the ceiling of buildings. Special requirements called for in specifications for stampings included smoothness and cleanliness to expedite further finishing in the Dublin plant, and close adherence to tolerances to permit tight fit in installation. Berlin had no experience with stampings of this type and determined to make a careful study of suppliers before making any major commitment.

Berlin also had a number of discussions with Anderson, with whom he had had an excellent relationship for a number of years. Both were aware of their limited experience with the special type of stampings to be bought for the new line, and agreed that they would, at least initially, depend heavily on potential suppliers for advice and assistance.

After a concentrated study of the technical aspects of stampings (including an analysis of the components of a competitor's unit) Berlin began calling in suppliers. Several of them were helpful in offering suggestions when Berlin told them frankly of his lack of experience. Berlin reviewed the quotations of about six of the suppliers, considered their willingness to offer technical advice and service, and decided to narrow the field to three. The bids were not far apart, and all were within reasonable competitive range.

Following his custom with major suppliers to the electrical division, Berlin decided to visit each of the three stamping plants, in company with the Superintendent and new Foreman. Because he wished to see the plants in normal operation, he made arrangements for his visits by telephone, only one day in advance. This, he felt, would give the suppliers little or no time to cover up major deficiencies in their facilities. None of the three companies seemed to resent this tactic and all three welcomed his visits.

Berlin was somewhat surprised on his visit to Company A, acknowledged as one of the leaders in the field, to find a rather old building and a number of old presses among the many new machines. Building and machines, were clean and well kept, and despite obviously high production, there were no signs of sloppiness, poor maintenance, or slow-downs because of insufficient equipment.

During the tour of the plant, the company's Sales engineer was joined by two men from the technical staff. They pointed out new deep-drawing equipment that produced better finishes on the stampings and an elaborate inspection set-up for controlling quality. Throughout, they demonstrated an alert, progressive attitude and an interest in helping Dublin with its technical and procurement problems. Company A's bid was slightly higher than those of the other two suppliers.

Company B was in a brand-new plant, laid out for straight-line production. It was clean, well-lit, and almost completely equipped with new presses and other machinery. Berlin noted that it apparently was not operating at full capacity. He was impressed by the skill of the machine operators and foremen and their willingness and ability to answer his and the Superintendent's technical questions promptly. Company B's Purchasing Manager was in the executive group that welcomed Berlin. He showed them the equipment that would be used on Dublin's order if the business were placed with his company.

Just before the entire party was ready to leave for lunch at a nearby restaurant, the Purchasing Manager asked Berlin and the Superintendent to examine the raw materials stockroom. It was spacious, well-stocked and well-equipped with a variety of materials-handling devices. A lorry load of steel sheet was being unloaded at the time, and he showed them the receiving procedure, which included sampling of standard acceptance tests applied to each lot.

Company C was the lowest bidder. It had a mixture of both old and new equipment all of which appeared to be working at top speed. Both men and materials seemed to be moving at a rapid pace and the foreman, who took the party through was very polite but preoccupied. Several times he was called away to answer telephone calls or to discuss various matters with machine operators. He did, however, spend a good deal of time explaining the company's inspection and quality-control procedure, a feature which was 100% inspection of all parts.

At the end of the tour he turned Berlin and the Superintendent over to the General Manager, who invited them out to lunch.

Task

Who should be awarded the contract and why?

6.   Procurement Methods

Introduction

This chapter will examine call-off contracts and negotiated procurement. There will also be brief consideration of the time taken to learn new techniques and change from previously used practices.

Framework Agreement

This framework agreement relates to unspecified quantities over a stated contract period for use by the purchaser:

THIS FRAMEWORK AGREEMENT is made the _____
day of _____

BETWEEN:-

(1) The **purchaser**; and
(2) **Supplier** whose registered office is at **address of Supplier** ('the Supplier').

WHEREAS:-

(A) An advertisement was placed by the **purchaser** in the Official Journal of the European Communities on 1 November 2005, reference (-) in respect of a framework agreement for the provision of supply of training services to the **purchaser** (as defined below) and from the expressions of interest received, it subsequently shortlisted a number of potential suppliers (including the Supplier) to participate in a competitive tender.

(B) On 1 March 2006 the **purchaser** invited the shortlisted suppliers (including the Supplier) to submit offers in respect of the procurement subject to the terms of the various documents comprising or included with the Invitation to Offer.

(C) On the basis of its offer, the **purchaser** has selected the Supplier (and may have appointed other suppliers) to provide training services (as defined below) to the **purchaser** in the manner and on the terms described herein.

In this example, definitions of the aspects of the contract mentioned, such as training services and full names and addresses were attached.

Call off Contracts

Definition

'A type of purchase order issued to a supplier covering the ongoing supply of material for a period of time, usually, but by no means always, one year'.

Usually, general quantity requirements over the stated time period will be provided by the buyer, but not detailed delivery timing. This information is forwarded to the supplier as it becomes available to the buyer.

Example

This order covers the supply of:

Widgets price £1.00 each

Estimated annual usage: 24000

Delivery instructions: to be called off as necessary

Forecast monthly usage: between 1000 and 3000

Notes: The following points are worthy of note regarding call-off contracts:

The phrase 'to be called off as necessary' may be perceived, by some suppliers, as being too vague. This may lead to situations where, when a quantity of the item is called off for urgent delivery, the supplier is unable to react to the buyer's requested delivery time because of the time required to make and deliver the item. The problem is that an estimated annual or monthly usage figure is not a contractual commitment unless the terms and conditions of the order state that it should be regarded as such. The problem, in this instance, for the buyer is that he/she might be committed to accept and pay for quantities of material that, in the event, are not required.

To counteract this potential problem some buyers send schedules, either electronically or by 'hard copy', to provide firm quantity commitments for each week/ month, depending on how the buyer requires deliveries. Buyers, in this instance, would usually insert a term in their call-off orders stating that quantities shown for (e.g.) the current month plus three months are a firm commitment. In respect of the quantities shown for the three months after this, the buyer will pay for the supplier's raw material purchases but not for work done by the supplier. Any quantities shown for months after this are a guide only and represent no commitment by the buyer. This process gives the supplier a chance to make timely raw material purchases and commence work so that the buyer's delivery expectations may be met.

The time allowed, under the above type of arrangement, as a firm commitment depends on:

Uses of call-off contracts

A call-off contract could be used to good effect when:

- General requirements for the time period can be assessed (e.g. forecast of between 500 and 1500 per month) but actual usage within the time period is not known precisely. There is irregular usage with no repeated pattern.

- Requirements may be fairly regular but storage space is very limited. Quantities may be called off as space becomes available.

- A range of maintenance, repair and operational (MRO) items may be available from one supplier with attractive discounts. For example, it may be beneficial to purchase all janitorial supplies (soap, towels, toilet rolls, etc.) from one supplier. One call-off contract to cover all the items would have the effect of securing the supply with reduced administration, as well as potentially giving a favourable discount across the range of items.

Once call-off contracts, typically for MRO items, have been set up with a supplier, a system of direct requisitioning may be used. Here, the user department(s) calls off their requirements, as necessary, using the call-off contract established by procurement. This saves the buyer from having to carry out much administrative work. While it may appear that, in this instance, the buyer is relinquishing the procurement process to the user department, this is not the case. Procurement source the supplier and negotiate the contract, all the user department is doing is calling off their requirements on a regular basis. The buyer does not need to carry out this task, indeed, if the buyer were looking after all call-offs, there would be little time for any other activities.

Features of call-off contracts

The following are important features of call-off contracts:

- They are particularly suitable for large organisations with centralised procurement who can take advantage of large volume discounts.

- They may be facilitated by electronic systems. An increasingly popular idea is for suppliers to have electronic access to the buyer's stock records (as far as they relate to the items supplied by that supplier) so that the supplier may 'manage' the buyer's inventory and re-supply automatically. This process is known as 'consignment stocking' or 'vendor managed inventory'. At a simpler level, schedules may be sent to suppliers electronically in order to call off quantities of items.

- Suppliers are guaranteed a specified volume of purchases although, usually, estimates of requirements are provided. Higher prices may be paid if actual usage falls below the estimate.

- Suppliers may build in price increases to cover the risk of a low rate of call off if there is no provision for price adjustment.

Benefits of call-off contracts

- Enables more strategic activity to be pursued. If the buyer is not careful, he/she may become 'bogged down' in placing orders for small quantities of material. Call-off orders, particularly if accompanied by direct requisitioning, may allow the buyer to concentrate on the strategic activities he/she is employed primarily to carry out.

- Reduce costs, particularly ordering costs. If a separate order were placed, instead of calling-off items, the annual ordering cost would escalate greatly. It should be remembered that ordering costs of £60.00 per order are not uncommon and this figure can escalate to £250.00 in some organisations. Often, when MRO items are purchased, the cost of placing the order can outweigh the cost of the goods.

☐ Decreases frequency of competitive bidding. Call-off contracts should ideally be awarded after a competitive bidding process but this process is costly and time-consuming and the award of a call-off contract can mean that it is only necessary once a year for each item or category of items.

☐ Facilitates continuity of supply. The estimates, particularly if accompanied by schedules, should allow the supplier to plan supplies. This is particularly true in the case of consignment stocking or vendor managed inventory.

☐ Minimises inventory levels. Call-offs may be made very regularly for small quantities, thus giving frequent stock turnover and low inventory levels.

☐ Results in less administrative and clerical activity, particularly if direct requisitioning is used.

Negotiated Procurement

Definition of negotiation

'A process designed to reconcile two or more different opinions in order that appropriate actions may be initiated or continued in mutually satisfying conditions.'

The intention here is to provide a guide as to the basic elements of the negotiation process and to compare negotiated procurement with the competitive bidding approach. Negotiating can include:

☐ Preparation.

☐ Proposing.

☐ Discussion.

☐ Bargaining.

☐ Agreeing.

☐ Confirming.

Negotiation can be an expensive and time-consuming process, so it is useful to consider the conditions necessary for effective negotiation:

☐ A scarce resource or a perceived need – competitive bidding may not be possible if a resource is scarce because there may not be enough suppliers to allow use of the technique.

☐ An intention of both sides to achieve an agreement – if there is no willingness to achieve an agreement, negotiation will not work.

☐ The ability to vary the terms – if there is no scope for either party to vary the terms, there will be no ability to concede and negotiation will not work.

Your ability to persuade another person to do something you want them to do is almost entirely dependent on their perception of your willingness to help them meet their needs. There are certain basic elements that are necessary to ensure the successful outcome of negotiation. These are described as follows:

Negotiation basics

☐ **Correct agenda** – it is essential to have an agenda for the meeting agreed by both parties.

☐ **Authority** – it is useful to ensure the authority levels of both the buyer and his/her opposite number. This is the extent to which either party to the negotiation can 'bind' their company.

☐ **Home ground** – most writers agree that it is best to try to ensure that the negotiation takes place on the buyer's 'home ground'.

☐ **Concessions and compromise** – it will be necessary to do this at some point. Try to ensure that you do not make the first concession and that any concession made is met with an equal concession from the other party.

☐ **Keep the initiative** – try to avoid being driven onto the defensive.

☐ **Equality 60/40** – this does not always mean equal in terms of 50/50. It means that both sides are satisfied with the outcome.

Use questions

☐ What?

☐ Who?

☐ When?

◻   Why?

◻   How?

The Negotiation Process

Negotiation moves through a number of clearly defined phases. These may be considered alongside the development process.

The Negotiation Development Process

Objectives

↓

Risk and reward

↓

Preparation and profiles

↓

SWOT

↓

Strategy, tactics and postures

↓

Negotiations

↓

Agreement

Many writers take the view that good preparation is the most important element of this process. This will now be examined.

Preparation stage

◻   Objectives set

◻   Research undertaken

◻   Strategy + tactics decided

◻   Cost analysis

◻   SWOT

◻   Profiles

These will now be examined in more detail.

Objectives set – the practice of using the MIL (Must, Intend, Like) is useful here. This enables the buyer to determine objectives in terms of:

- **Must** – those that must be achieved (failure to do so would result in 'walking away').

- **Intend** – those that the buyer intends to achieve. These are not as important as the 'M' objectives but are useful to achieve.

- **Like** – these are the 'icing on the cake'. If the buyer achieves a significant proportion of these, he/she would have been very successful. These objectives are the first ones to be conceded, should concession be necessary.

Research undertaken – research should be undertaken to determine such things as:

- the relative strengths/weaknesses of both buyer and seller.

- how the product under discussion is processed – what raw materials are used, what threats to supply there are or might be.

- whether the supplier is a market leader or 'follower'.

- how badly the supplier wants the buyer's business.

- how certain the supplier is of gaining the buyer's business.

Strategy and tactics decided: This is summarised in the following negotiating strategy table.

Adversarial	Collaborative
Competitive	Partnership
Win/lose	Win/win
Conflict	Co-operative
Lack of trust	Trust
Closed book	Open book
Short-term view	Long-term view

Cost analysis – a full cost analysis of the product or service under discussion should be carried out to identify such aspects as the raw material cost, supplier's profit margin, etc.

SWOT

Profiles – A negotiator's most important single responsibility in preparing for negotiation is to appraise his/her own strengths and weaknesses accurately in relation to the seller's strengths and weaknesses.

Negotiation Phases

The actual process of conducting negotiation, in terms of the meeting(s) may be described as follows:

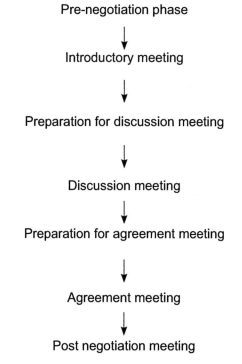

Pre-negotiation phase

↓

Introductory meeting

↓

Preparation for discussion meeting

↓

Discussion meeting

↓

Preparation for agreement meeting

↓

Agreement meeting

↓

Post negotiation meeting

The 'win/win' approach

There is much written today about the benefits of the 'win/win' approach to negotiation, the view being that a collaborative approach is taken by both parties. The end result should be that both parties come out of the negotiation process feeling that they have gained something.

If there is any doubt about this approach, it should be remembered that a supplier who gains little or nothing out of the negotiation process will not be committed to give the buyer the advanced levels of service often sought by buyers today. The main features of the win/win approach are:

- **Common objectives** – it is likely that both parties will have similar objectives, such as mutual success.

- **Mutuality** – the idea of mutual success and mutual interest in the outcome of negotiation should be stressed.

- **Free flow of information** – there should be no attempt to hide information. Transparency of such information as cost and technology information is considered important.
- **Empowerment**

- **Trust** – there should be an attempt by the buyer to develop mutual trust.

- **Benchmarking** – this may be used as a measure to ascertain the benefits of the arrangement resulting from the negotiation.

Negotiation skills and errors

Negotiation skills may be summarised as:

- communication.

- analysis.

- listening.

- commercial acumen.

- pragmatic approach.

- long- and short-term perspective.

Some of these focus on the interpersonal and communication skills of the buyer. Others, such as 'analysis', emphasise the buyer's ability to prepare prior to the negotiation meeting(s).

Errors in negotiation

Major errors generally include:

- **Lack of preparation** – emphasised earlier.

- **Too many concessions** – considered earlier, try to avoid making the first one.

- **Revealing bottom line** – whilst openness is considered a positive thing, it should be remembered that too much will put the buyer in a position where there is no room to manoeuvre.

- **Meeting** 'half way'.

- **Lack of knowledge** – the buyer's preparation should provide insight into how the product is made, from what, etc.

- **Over-confidence.**

- **Lack of authority** – the buyer should ensure that he/she has sufficient authority to enter into the negotiation and 'bind' his/her company.

- **Conceding** too early.

- **One-way** concessions.

- **Poor/weak openings** – communication skills are important.

- **Adversarial stance** – the opposite of the win/win approach.

Comparison of negotiated procurement with competitive tendering

Many buyers tend to use competitive bidding/tendering as a means of ensuring that they obtain the 'best' deal from suppliers. The theory behind this practice is that the tendering process will 'stimulate the competitive pressures' that exist in the supply market such that every supplier who submits a tender will submit their best price and other terms. Thus, when the buyer selects the 'best' tenderer, he/she will automatically obtain the best deal.

There are, however, flaws in this theory. Firstly, competitive tendering can only work properly if a number of pre-requisites are met.

- There are sufficient suppliers in the supply market. Also, tenders need to be sent to an adequate number of them. If an item/material is scarce, this condition will almost certainly not apply.

- All suppliers must actively want to bid. If some do not, the process is undermined.

☐ The spend on the item/material must be large enough to attract suppliers to submit a quotation. If not, again, the process will be undermined.

☐ The Request for Proposal (RFP) details must be clear and unambiguous. If not, suppliers are likely to 'pad' their quotations to cover unforeseen eventualities. Again, in this instance, the process will be undermined.

☐ There must be sufficient time for suppliers to complete quotations and submit them. If not, comments under RFP details above will apply.

If any of these pre-requisite conditions is not present for whatever reason, the competitive tendering process is doomed to failure. In this event, the buyer will need to consider the use of negotiation as a means of selecting the 'best' supplier and obtaining the 'best' deal. There are other strong arguments against competitive tendering:

☐ The lowest-price supplier may be forced to cut quality to achieve the quoted price.

☐ The winning tenderer often removes competition from the marketplace and, consequently, achieves a monopoly position that can threaten the buyer in future.

☐ The difficulties, expense and time associated with switching to new suppliers.

Advantages of negotiation

☐ Reduced time spent looking for new suppliers and gathering competitive bids.

☐ Continuity of relationships with suppliers who are aware of your needs and way of doing business. This pre-supposes that:

- the organisation has dealt with the supplier for some time.
- they are 'tried and tested'.
- there is some form of partnership arrangement with the supplier.
- Incentives for suppliers to invest in electronic and manufacturing systems compatible with those of the customer organisation. Examples include Electronic Data Interchange (EDI) to allow the supplier to access inventory information.

There are, however, some disadvantages attached to negotiation, although these are kept to a minimum if the process is carried out correctly.

☐ Increased danger of collusion and fraud.

☐ Increased difficulty of evaluating offers on an equal basis.

☐ No guarantee that the outcome of the negotiation will be competitive in relation to the supply market.

To summarise, if carried out correctly, following the guidelines given above, negotiation can be used to great effect to select the 'right' supplier. In order for negotiation to work adequately with unknown suppliers, extensive supplier evaluation should be carried out first so that the buyer is dealing with known supplier capabilities.

Negotiation and competitive tendering are not mutually exclusive: post-tender negotiation is widely used by buyers to finalise deals that have been set in motion using competitive tendering.

Food for thought

Are there any situations in your organisation where competitive tendering is not working to give you a satisfactory deal? Could negotiation be used to good effect to give a satisfactory deal? If so, how would you prepare for the negotiation?

Chapter Summary

In this chapter a number of 'modern' procurement methods have been examined.

These include:

☐ Call-off contracts and the circumstances in which their use may be beneficial

☐ Negotiated procurement, including how it should be carried out and a comparison with the technique of competitive tendering.

Case Study

Saran Fashions Ltd

Mr Johnson is the Assistant Purchasing Manager for Saran Fashions Ltd., a large multiple chain of fashion shops specialising in low cost fashions for women, aimed at between 18 and 30. The key marketing strategy of the company is simply 'keep it cheap and cheerful', low-prices and bright colours".

The company has been in business since the mid 1960s and has grown steadily. The market for this type of product is very competitive, and there are several other chains in the high street who offer a similar product range. The Senior Management of the company have recently formulated a corporate plan for the next 3 years, its main aim is to protect the company's market share and hopefully bring about a slight increase, at the expense of its main rivals.

The contribution of purchasing to this objective is clearly stated in a memo sent to Mr Johnson by the Managing Director, (see Appendix 1) to reduce prices paid for its supplies. Mr Johnson is very unhappy with this strategy. He feels that this kind of pressure on suppliers to reduce prices only results in poor supplier relationships and, in the final analysis, a poor service. He decides to make an appointment to go and see Dawn Wood at Fairfield Dress Manufacturers. She is the founder of the company and has dealt with Saran Fashions for some time.

Fairfield Dress Manufacturers are a very small outfit operating in the East End of London. It employs about 20 people in all. Dawn Wood started the business at home some five years ago. She has built the business up virtually on her own. Ms Wood knows her business and she knows the market place. There are a large number of small dress manufacturers in East London, many of them only just break-even. The past couple of years have been very difficult. Low cost imports from South East Asia are partly to blame, coupled with a general recession in the high street. Mr Johnson has decided to meet with Ms Wood because he has always had a very good working relationship with her.

Fairfield have always produced good quality products with reliable delivery and fair prices. Mr Johnson feels sure that Ms Wood will be able to reduce her prices by some degree. Andy Tyson is an Assistant Buyer for Saran Fashions and he reports directly to Mr Johnson. Mr Tyson has been asked to produce a report concerning Fairfield. It was meant to be ready for the coming meeting but it seems that it will not now be available. Mr Johnson is not too upset by this. He feels he knows Dawn well enough not to need it. Andy offers to give him a verbal briefing, but Mr Johnson declines. He states "I know Dawn, she'll be happy to help out with this price cutting idea". A few days later Mr. Johnson visits Ms Wood at her factory. Following the normal greetings the two get down to business.

Ms Wood: "What can I do you for Ben?"

Mr Johnson: "It's this stupid Corporate Plan I was telling you about. I am very sorry but I must ask for a price reduction."

Ms Wood: "You must be joking! Our prices are rock bottom as it is".

Mr Johnson: "It's not my idea, Dawn".

Ms Wood: "I should hope not. Just think of the service we give you, delivery on time, only a 10% reject rate and all at good prices".

Mr Johnson: "Yes I know what a good supplier you are. If it were up to me I wouldn't be asking".

Ms Wood: "A price cut is out of the question Ben and that's final".

Mr Johnson: "I've got to have something for the Board, otherwise they may force me to source from somebody new".

Ms Wood: "Let's look at this item, code 146. Now at the moment, you sell that in your store for just over £16.00 and yet you buy it from us at only £8.25".

Mr Johnson: "Yes, we do make a good profit on that line, but others only just break even, I think".

Ms Wood: "Look, all I can offer is faster delivery. It means my workshop working overtime, maybe but, well, you are a good customer".

Mr Johnson: "That's very good of you. Our stock control people are always complaining about the problems of late delivery".

Appendix 1

Memo

From	:	Managing Director
To	:	Ben Johnson
Subject	:	Purchasing

The only way that we can stay in this business and hopefully expand, is by an overall reduction in the prices we pay for our stock. Every % reduction that can be achieved equals an increase in profits. It is your task to negotiate with our suppliers to reduce their prices.

Winston James
Managing Director

Tasks

Evaluate Mr Johnson's performance as a negotiator under headings:

1.   Preparation

2.   Tactics

3.   Objectives

7.   Strategic Partnerships and Outsourcing

Introduction

Definition of Strategic Partnerships

'A commitment by customer/suppliers, regardless of size, to a long-term relationship based on clear mutually agreed objectives to strive for world-class capability and performance'.

(Confederation of British Industry)

The basic concept of partnership sourcing leads to the buyer developing a collaborative relationship with 'tried and tested' suppliers, usually on a single-source basis, rather than constantly using competitive tendering as a basis for re-awarding contracts. For many buyers this involves a radical departure from the traditional view of purchasing characterised by:

☐   dual or multiple sourcing of all major/critical items or services.

☐   extensive use of competitive tendering to award contracts in the first place and to re-award them on an ongoing basis.

☐   short-term contracts.

☐   adversarial or 'arm's-length' relationships.

The characteristics of partnership have been defined as follows:

☐   **Top level commitment** – partnerships cannot work without management being committed to their success.

☐   **Openness and trust** – most writers on the subject emphasise the need for mutual trust, a concept some buyers find problematic.

☐   **Clear joint objectives** between buyer and supplier – the emphasis is on working together to achieve mutual objectives.

☐   **Long-term relationship** – partnerships take time to develop and will not develop if it is obvious that the buyer will move to another supplier 'at the drop of a hat'.

☐   **Proactive not reactive** – partnerships will not simply 'happen', they need to be made to happen and to succeed.

☐   **Total Quality Management (TQM)** – there is much emphasis on the partner supplier working proactively towards quality achievement/ improvement.

☐   **Working together.**

☐   **Flexibility** – working to solve problems as they occur.

☐   **Involvement of all disciplines** – the emphasis is not merely on a relationship between Procurement and the supplier's sales department but on horizontal relationships at all levels and, where necessary, between all departments. Thus, for example, the technical departments in both organisations would be encouraged to collaborate.

A. Erridge – ('Managing Purchasing'
Butterworth Heinemann)

Advantages for buyers

These advantages may be summarised by saying that an effective partnership will allow the buyer to achieve advanced levels of quality and service that would never be possible under the adversarial approach. Such service levels include:

☐ faster product and service development.

☐ a commitment by the supplier to quality improvement and technical development.

☐ delivery on time.

☐ a commitment by the supplier to design cost out.

Advantages for the supplier

☐ Long-term agreement.

☐ Improved management capability.

☐ Marketing advantage.

☐ Improved technological capability.

☐ Financial stability including payment on time.

Advantages for both parties

☐ Reduced total cost, profitable for both parties.

☐ Lower inventories and reduced logistics.

Thus, there would appear to be a number of advantages to the concept of supplier partnerships. However, it cannot be stressed too much that, to be successful, a partnership must be implemented properly.

To this end, *Ellram's model (1991)* is useful, see overleaf:

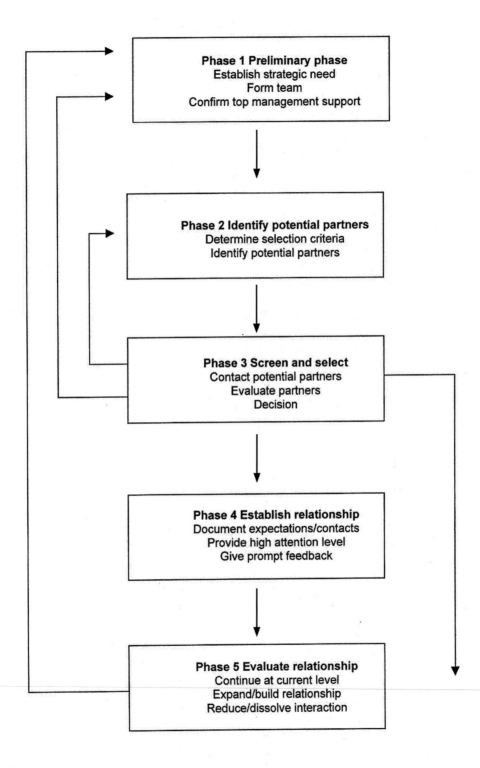

In more detail, Ellram's phases may be described as follows.

Phase 1 Preliminary phase

- Identify need for partnership as part of the organisation's strategic plan.

- A team representing key functional areas works on the development of the partnership.

- Top management support must be confirmed.

Phase 2 Identify potential partners

- Determine the selection criteria – these may include: cultural compatibility, long-term plans, financial stability, technology/ design capability, top management compatibility, location, local laws and tariffs (foreign partners), plant visits - may be necessary to confirm some of these.

- Identify potential partners.

Phase 3 Screen and select

Potential suppliers are rated against the selection criteria and their commitment to the partnership ideals identified. Selection should not be dominated by any single criterion but should seek an overall balance between them.

Phase 4 Establish the relationship

The partners' expectations of the relationship should be documented to prevent misunderstandings. This should include:

- key contacts.

- shared technology.

- handling of proprietary information.

- frequency of forecast updates.

- basis for price change.

Procurement should provide a central co-ordinating function with regular team meetings to evaluate performance.

Phase 5 Evaluate relationships

After an initial period of (e.g.) 12 months, the performance of the relationship may be evaluated with possible outcomes being:

- maintain at the present level.

- further build or expand the relationship.

- dissolve or reduce the scope of the relationship (a decision not to be taken lightly).

Lastly, it should be remembered that strategic partnerships must work, ideally for both parties:

'Co-operation and alliances endure only as long as there is mutual competitive advantage. Organisations do not co-operate in order to be nice to each other, but to create advantage'.

Strategic partnerships are not the only viable type of relationship. In terms of what kind of relationship the buyer should adopt with suppliers, the following matrix, developed by DPSS Consultants, is useful.

The differences between traditional relationships and more collaborative ones may be summarised in the table overleaf.

Traditional	Collaborative
Arm's length	Partnership
Adversarial	Co-operative
Negotiating price	Co-managing costs
Limited contact	Broad involvement
Problem solving	Prevention
Incoming inspection	Process control
Gatekeeper	Facilitator
Contract-based	Trust + performance
Short-term	Long-term
Win/lose	Win/win

Outsourcing

Definition

'The strategic use of resources to perform activities traditionally handled by internal staff and their resources....[It is a] management strategy by which an organisation out-sources major non-core functions to specialised, efficient service providers'.

C.K. Lysons ('Purchasing and Supply Chain Management' Prentice Hall)

Examples of outsourced activities include, but are not limited to:

☐ cleaning.

☐ building repairs and maintenance.

☐ catering.

☐ security.

☐ transport management.

    ☐   waste disposal.

    ☐   reception.

    ☐   pest control.

    ☐   training.

    ☐   computers and information technology (IT).

There are three basic types of outsourcing.

    ☐   **'Body shop' outsourcing** – a situation where management uses outsourcing as a means of meeting short-term requirements such as a shortage of in-house skills to meet temporary demand.

    ☐   **Project management outsourcing** – is employed for all or part of a particular project, e.g. developing a new IT project, training in new skills, etc.

    ☐   **Total outsourcing** – where the service provider is given full responsibility for a selected area, e.g. catering, security.

Benefits of outsourcing

There are a number of perceived benefits of outsourcing.

    ☐   **Frees management time** to concentrate on 'core' activities – businesses need to ask questions such as 'what business are we in?' and focus on that activity.

    ☐   **Reduced staff costs** – there is no need to employ staff to provide the service 'in-house'.

    ☐   **Increased flexibility** – outsourced services may be increased/decreased/altered without the need for employing staff or getting rid of staff.

    ☐   **Cost certainty** – a fee is paid (weekly, monthly, etc.) to the service provider. This does not change as long as the service remains constant and allows efficient budgeting.

- **Reduction in staff management problems** – the organisation will have fewer employees to manage directly.

- **Improved consistency** of service.

- **Reduced capital requirements** – there is no need to acquire the capital equipment needed to support a service (e.g. vehicles). Also, existing capital equipment may be disposed of if the service for which it is required is outsourced, thus making capital funds available.

- **Gain access to world-class capabilities** – based on the assumption that the service provider is an expert in their field. This is considered very important by many buyers.

Implementing outsourcing

This involves the following stages.

- Set up a team to consider the strategic need to outsource, including reasons, cost comparisons between in-house provision and anticipated benefits/problems.

- Prepare an appropriate specification for the service – this is considered very important.

- Consider possible suppliers.

- Invite tenders against the specification.

- Evaluate the tenders against pre-determined evaluation criteria.

- Carry out post-tender negotiation, as necessary.

- Award the contract, including a service level agreement.

- Set up a management control and monitoring process.

Problems of outsourcing

'You can outsource the activity but not the responsibility.'

Ray Carter

Outsourcing is not without potential disadvantages, although the occurrence and effects of these may be reduced by developing a specification and negotiating a service-level agreement with the chosen contractor.

The problems may be summarised as follows:

- dependence on a few suppliers.

- the quality of the service may be variable.

- co-ordination of different suppliers.

- lack of supplier flexibility.

- over-dependence on suppliers.

- lack of management skills to control suppliers.

Additionally, many writers hold the view that 'core' activities should never be outsourced, nor should any activities that give the organisation a competitive advantage or a distinctive competence.

The problem here is that it can be difficult to establish what exactly a 'core' activity is. In Rothery, B and Robinson (*'The Truth about Outsourcing'*), Gower states that the following activities should not be outsourced:

- management of strategic planning.

- management of finances.

- management of management consultancy.

- control of supplies.

- quality and environmental management.

- supervision of the meeting of regulatory requirements such as product liability, misleading advertising, quality, health and safety, etc.

Food for thought

Are there any services currently provided in-house in your organisation that could be outsourced? What are they?

Learning Curve

It should be noted that the implementation of all the concepts considered in this chapter will require learning by buyers and other staff, including management. This is because the implementation of all these concepts takes time and cannot happen 'overnight'.

None of these concepts could be implemented instantly and all involve new processes. Thus, it has to be recognised that, for the implementation of these concepts to be successful in the long-term, a 'learning curve' approach needs to be adopted. This will involve:

☐   learning about the concepts.

☐   learning how to implement them.

☐   learning about potential pitfalls and how to avoid them.

☐   recognising that change takes time.

☐   recognising that some financial investment may be needed to get the concepts started.

Chapter Summary

In this chapter a number of 'modern' procurement methods have been examined. These include:

☐   call-off contracts and the circumstances in which their use may be beneficial.

☐   negotiated procurement, including how it should be carried out and a comparison with the technique of competitive tendering.

☐   strategic partnerships, their advantages and disadvantages and how they may be implemented in practice.

☐   outsourcing including its benefits and drawbacks and methodology for its successful implementation.

☐   the learning necessary for buyers to be able to implement all the above concepts and techniques.

Case Study

Managing Strategic Contracting Decisions

Delta Ltd is a large manufacturing company producing a range of very well-known machines for the oil and gas market, UK and the Gulf. It has a turnover of over £10 million per annum. Recently it has designed and developed a new generation of high-tech machines, which employs the latest technology and the unique selling proposition of being able to operate using only 30 per cent of the energy consumed by traditional models; it also has a unique control system to reduce the amount of materials needed to achieve excellent results.

Jane Tilly, Director of Marketing, feels Delta has a winning product, providing it can establish itself in the marketplace, gaining the acceptance of sceptical customers and the trade. Reliability and cost are the vital elements. A well-known advertising agency is handling promotion of the product; a key theme of the campaign will be 'total reliability'.

The Director of Contracting is Susan French, who recently joined the business from a rival company in Italy. Susan has an MBA from a famous UK business school and is a professionally qualified buyer. She thinks the company must improve its approach to sourcing. Her experience working in Italy has convinced her that any improvements in quality, design and total acquisition costs can be greatly improved by more innovative and professional strategic sourcing; concepts such as Strategic Partnerships needs to be introduced to achieve these improvements.

Delta has a large contracting department, run on very traditional lines. Contracts are awarded on the principle of lowest price and are carefully constructed in an effort to eliminate any chance of the suppliers avoiding their responsibilities, as some have tried to do in the past. There are three main contracting divisions. Head of Equipment Contracting, Jim Peterson, began in the engineering department and steadily worked up to senior management. He likes telling new members of his team: "I got where I am today by not making mistakes".

One of the key elements in any machine is the auto feed control unit, in the industry it is widely known that 95per cent of all equipment failures and breakdowns can be attributed to faults in this key component. Obviously the sourcing of this item is fundamental to the success of the product. As the managing director of the company has said in a memo to the production manager, the future of the company is staked on the new product.

Traditionally, the auto feed control unit used in Delta's machines have been from the UK market - in particular Omega Ltd. Jim Peterson has already suggested that the contract for the auto feed control unit be placed with Omega, a locally-based manufacturing company employing about 100 people. Unemployment in the area is quite high and the current recession has hit the company hard: in recent years Omega has reduced its R&D expenditure and cut back on several major investment programmes. Delta has a corporate strategy, part of which is to support local industry and the local community. The company has sponsored several education and training programmes in conjunction with the local community.

Omega has suffered from quality problems in the past and has had to employ inspectors and checkers to reduce the number of faulty products leaving the factory. Jim Peterson feels sure that with an extra tight contract and improved inspection and checking procedures at Delta's end, he will be able to ensure the consistency of quality. And of course Omega is very competitive on price (up to 10 per cent cheaper than its new rival, SKS), a vital factor in the traditional Contracting decision.

Susan French, on the other hand, takes a different view. In recent times the improved quality and competitive price of several South Korean suppliers has called the traditional sourcing decision into question. One supplier in particular, the SKS Corporation, which has recently established a sales office in London and has a very good reputation in the marketplace, is well-known for their quality.

Jim and Susan have crossed swords on several occasions regarding sourcing decisions. Jim thinks that Susan does not understand the realities of the situation; Omega is a well-known company which has worked closely with Delta. Susan feels that Jim is too conservative and that a more proactive approach would reap great quality and price rewards. She is determined to use SKS.

At a recent meeting to discuss the issue, the Managing Director had to step in to restore order as Susan and Jim got into a heated debate. Jane Tilly brought them back to earth by pointing out: "The key issue is not whether Omega or SKS are acceptable to us; it's whether they are acceptable to our customers."

The sourcing decision is vital to Delta's future. It must be made in light of this, and take into account the cost of having to go through the process again should the decision be less than optimal.

Task

Analyse the situation and make recommendations regarding the most appropriate procurement strategy.

8. Technology and E-Procurement

Introduction

This chapter will examine aspects of the use of technology in procurement and e-commerce and, specifically, will cover the use of computers in procurement, information systems, efficiency improvements through technology, and e-procurement and e-commerce applications.

Glossary Of Key Terms

Bar coding

This is a form of automatic identification widely used to capture data from (e.g.) product packages and very widely used in warehouses for stock coding purposes.

E-business

A wider process than e-commerce. E-commerce relates to transactions whereas e-business relates to a wide range of production, customer and internal processes only indirectly related to commercial transactions. It may provide such benefits as:

☐   provision of 24/7 information access.

☐   aggregation of information from several sources.

☐   accurate audit trails of transactions, enabling businesses to identify the areas of the business offering the greatest potential for efficiency improvements and cost reductions.

☐   personalisation and customisation of information.

E-commerce

'Using an electronic network to simplify and speed up all stages of the business process, from design and making to buying and delivery, e-commerce is the exchange of information across electronic networks, at any stage in the supply chain, whether within an organisation, between businesses and consumers or between the public and private sectors, whether paid or unpaid.'

(Department of Trade and Industry)

E-procurement

The business-to-business purchase and sale of supplies and services over the Internet.

Electronic data interchange (EDI)

'The technique based on agreed standards, which facilitates business transactions in standardised electronic form in an automated manner directly from a computer application in one organisation to an application in another.'

C. K. Lysons: ('Purchasing and Supply Chain Management' – Prentice Hall)

This may otherwise be described as the linking of computers between specific organisations so that documents, such as purchase orders and invoices, may be transmitted directly by electronic means.

Electronic Point of Sale (EPOS)

Electronic Point of Sale (EPOS) is used widely in the retail sector and captures information that a sale has been made, resulting in a number of units of product being taken out of stock. This information is collated by the system, and the system automatically 'triggers' the re-ordering process by sending schedules electronically, either to a distribution centre owned by the retailer or directly to suppliers.

EPOS drives the whole re-ordering and stock replenishment process for major retailers with many branches. While it is used mainly in the retail sector, it has implications for other sectors, namely:

    ☐   vendor-managed inventory (VMI) – suppliers can track stock movement in their customers' facilities and can replenish stock automatically.

    ☐   assistance in collaborative planning, forecasting and replenishment.

Internet

A worldwide network (correctly a 'network of networks') accessible by telephone lines. The 'hardware that allows the WorldWide Web to operate.

Intranet

An organisation-wide system that operates like an internal Internet. It allows everyone in the organisation to share information and may provide the following benefits:

    ☐   publication of corporate documents such as policy statements.

    ☐   publication of individual documents for group discussion.

    ☐   providing consistent communication between colleagues.

Extranet

An Intranet that has been extended to include access to selected external organisations, such as customers or suppliers, to facilitate the communication and sharing of information.

Local area networks (LAN)

Privately owned communication networks linking PCs, workstations or telephones within a limited geographical area.

Metropolitan area networks (MAN)

Computer or telephone linking of two or more LANs within a limited geographical area.

Wide area networks (WAN)

These extend over a large geographical area such as a whole country.

Computer use in Procurement Management

There are a variety of uses, and actual uses of computers/IT will differ from organisation to organisation. Typical areas for consideration include the following.

Integrated databases/information systems including supply chain database containing the following:

☐ supplier index giving addresses, contacts, items supplied.

☐ vendor ratings.

☐ details of supplier visits.

☐ complete record of items purchased giving prices, suppliers, orders placed, etc.

☐ price trends of 'sensitive' commodities for monitoring purposes.

☐ records of material issued to subcontractors.

☐ records of jigs, tools, etc. owned by the purchaser but in possession of suppliers.

☐ contract records (i.e. 'blanket' orders).

☐ register of orders placed each day, cross-referenced against requisitions or any other relevant internal document (project, enquiry, etc.)

☐ usage/demand patterns.

☐ stock information.

☐ specifications.

Networking computers – e.g. linking your MRP system to that of suppliers via EDI.

Bar coding – printing these to assist storage/stock control.

EPOS – variants on this theme are increasingly being used in industries other than retail.

Online auctions – bids can be sought electronically from suppliers. Beware of timescales given to bidders. There is no set rule as to how much time each bidder is allowed in order to present further bids.

E-mail, Internet and e-commerce. *Chin Nam (1998)* gave the benefits of eprocurement as:

- □ reducing purchase cycle time.

- □ enhancing budgetary control.

- □ eliminating admin errors.

- □ increasing buyers' productivity.

- □ lowering prices through product standardisation and consolidation of procurement power.

- □ better information management.

- □ improving the payment process.

Food for thought

Consider your own procurement database, if one exists, and compare the information held on it with the information shown above. What, if any, information do you believe is missing?

Information Systems

Definition

'The means by which organisations and people utilising appropriate technologies gather, process, store, use and disseminate information'.

> *C. K. Lysons: ('Purchasing and Supply Chain Management' – Prentice Hall)*

Information systems may be classified as follows.

Transactional processing systems (TPS)

A transaction is any event that requires a record to be generated for evidence/ historical reasons, such as the placing of an order or processing of an invoice. Such data provides the basis for management reporting systems.

Management reporting systems (MRS)

These systems provide managers with information and support for effective decision making and provide feedback on daily operations. The information provided is usually in the form of reports generated through accumulated TPS. Typical procurement reports might include:

- value of orders placed in a specific period.

- value of orders to any one supplier.

- current expenditure or commitment against budgets.

- updated expenditure on capital projects.

- vendor rating reports.

- slow-moving and dead stocks.

It should be obvious that such information as shown above may be collated and presented in a manual format or by computer. The use of computers for such reporting is quicker, more accurate and can more easily be shown as trends.

Decision support systems (DSS)

These enable individuals or groups to make decisions by summarising all relevant information, whether held internally or externally, such as interest rates or currency changes. DSS have the following characteristics.

- They use both data and models (a representation of a system, process, etc. in mathematical form).

- They should assist managers in solving both structured and unstructured problems.

- They support rather than replace managerial judgement.

- Their objective is to improve the effectiveness of the decision rather than the efficiency with which the decision is made.

DSS tend to use either spreadsheets or expert systems. Spreadsheets are used widely to display figures or text and may be used to make calculations. Expert systems involve the user answering questions posed by a computer program and the program then reaching a diagnosis or solution to the problem.

Executive information systems (EIS)

An extension of DSS intended to provide current and appropriate information to support decision-making by executives. These systems emphasise the use of graphical displays, canned reports and briefings to save time. In many instances the above types of information system may be integrated through a common database.

At the most basic level, important procurement information is collected and collated at the following stages of the procurement cycle. Documentation relating to each stage may be generated manually or electronically.

- Requisition from user department.

- Requisition checked against user's budget/stock records.

- Enquiry (Request For Quotation [RFQ]) sent to potential suppliers.

- Quotations/expressions of interest/proposals received from potential suppliers.

- Negotiation/clarification followed by placing of purchase order.

- Advice note sent by supplier confirming delivery dates.

- When goods arrive they will be accompanied by a delivery note.

- Upon receipt of goods, a goods received note (GRN) will be completed and sent to departments such as Finance, Stores.

- Supplier sends invoice and, assuming it matches order and GRN, is paid.

Today, all these activities, where they involve communication, can be done electronically. An issue of great importance is the creation of an audit trail so that such matters as the justification for making the purchase can always be checked. To this end, once the system has been accessed at some point, there should be means of cross-referencing all the other stages in the cycle. For example, once a purchase order has been accessed, it should be possible, from cross-references contained in it, to access the original requisition and any enquiry and quotation work that has preceded it.

Food for thought

Consider the provision of information in your own organisation. In what ways, if any, does it differ from the above?

E-Procurement And E-Commerce Applications

Definitions

Both terms were defined in the glossary at the beginning of this chapter but, for ease of reference, will be repeated here:

E-commerce

'Using an electronic network to simplify and speed up all stages of the business process, from design and making to buying and delivery, e-commerce is the exchange of information across electronic networks, at any stage in the supply chain, whether within an organisation, between businesses and consumers or between the public and private sectors, whether paid or unpaid.'

(Department of Trade and Industry)

E-procurement

'The business-to-business purchase and sale of supplies and services over the Internet.'

E-procurement may be regarded as a subset of e-commerce (indeed, the terms are often used synonymously) and generally refers to the use of computers linked by networks (Internet, Intranet, Extranet) to perform any or all of the following functions.

- Access data relating to products available in the supply market.

- Find sources of supply and pre-qualify/appraise them.

- Make price comparisons or searches.

- Advertise the buyer's organisation's requirement.

- Issue invitations to tender and award contracts.

- Issue call-off orders.

- Buy from auction websites or market exchanges.

- Monitor supplier performance.

- Receive invoices and make payments.

- Act as a delivery channel for incoming services, such as consultancy or software.

☐ Provide for other general dealings with suppliers and supply markets, such as information gathering on legislative changes or research papers or reports.

E-procurement is also used widely for the purchase of Maintenance Repair and Operational (MRO) items. These largely low-value items can result in the buyer becoming 'swamped' by paperwork if purchased traditionally; automating paper-based processes can result in time savings and executive effort, and release procurement personnel to deal with more strategic issues.

Some organisations are currently attempting to extend e-procurement from MRO purchases to all 'mainstream' purchases.

Food for thought

How well developed is your organisation in terms of e-procurement? What future developments do you envisage it undertaking in this area?

Efficiency Improvements Through Technology

In general, the use of technology can make the capture, storage and retrieval of data more accurate, quicker and more reliable. Specifically, the following benefits have been claimed for the use of e-procurement.

☐ Reduced prices resulting from better sourcing and more competitive pressure.

☐ Shorter procurement cycle time due to better and quicker communication.

☐ Greater empowerment for line staff, who can order from their desktop PCs. This does not reduce the authority of the procurement function because it is they who will set up the contract for other staff to order against.

☐ Better and more accurate audit trail than with paper systems.

☐ Processes become more transparent, especially with the use of information systems.

☐ Fewer errors due to the nature of computer-based systems

ensuring that, if codes or data are incorrect, information will not be logged or transmitted.

☐ Procurement personnel are released to concentrate on strategic matters rather than paperwork.

☐ Reduced 'maverick buying' (the procurement of goods and services by non-procurement personnel without using official order forms or contracts). The way in which e- procurement systems are set up should mean that attempts at maverick buying are prevented by suppliers.

☐ Access to new suppliers, products and services.

☐ Tools such as e-auctions may attract new suppliers into the market.

Chapter Summary

This chapter has examined technology and e-commerce (specifically, e-procurement) and has included:

☐ a glossary of key terms to assist in the understanding of some of the basic issues considered here.

☐ the use of computers in procurement, covering such aspects as databases, networking computers, EPOS, e-auctions, etc.

☐ the different types of information system used in procurement.

☐ the nature and benefits of e-procurement, including efficiency improvements through its use.

9. Procurement of Services

Introduction

Contemporary procurement best practice in relation to products focuses on the following:

☐ the role of inventories.

☐ the achievement of just-in-time supply.

☐ the need for supply base reduction to facilitate the development of better working relationships with the chosen suppliers.

The question is whether these concepts can be applied to the procurement of services.

A Comparison Between Goods and Services

Major differences exist between the procurement of services and the procurement of products. The table opposite highlights some of the differences.

Service	Product
Intangible	Tangible
Not held in stock	Can be held in stock
Service often performed at the purchaser's premises	Products are delivered
Change of personnel can vary the quality of service	Output consistent
Standards can be difficult to establish and measure	Standards can be established and tests done to check conformance

Goods are usually tangible, e.g. you can physically touch a pump or drill bit. Services are usually intangible, although the results of the service may be seen.

Storage

By their nature, services cannot be stored. This means that they must be provided at a time which coincides exactly with the need.

Place

Products tend to be manufactured at a supplier's plant, and subsequently transported via the supply chain to the customers. A service will typically be performed at the purchaser's premises, for example:

- cleaning.

- transport.

- security.

- catering.

Role of People

Services are carried out by people. The content of the work depends on their inputs and care for the customer (the purchaser). The quality of goods, on the other hand, is reasonably evident. In services, the customer judges not only the outcome of the service, but also the way in which it was performed.

Standards

A product can be measured, weighed, tested and inspected to evaluate whether it conforms to the specification. Services, on the other hand, are more difficult to measure. The 'deliverables' of the service need to be defined. Most services have an output which can be assessed. For example, in a restaurant, the deliverables would be the meal. The same principle can be applied to any service contract.

There is a danger of seeing the procurement of goods or products and the procurement of services as two different things. However, analysis of a particular service should reveal that there is normally the combination of a mix of both goods and a service, see figure1 overleaf.

Type of producer

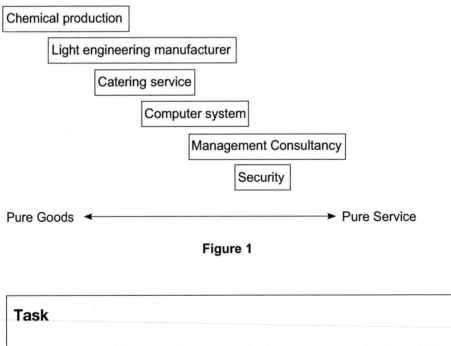

Figure 1

Task

Analyse one of the services bought by your organisation. What is the goods element and what is the service element?

The Key Principles of Buying Services

Defining the Requirement

The following key questions should be asked.

☐ What objectives and targets should be set?

☐ What benefits should the service provide?

☐ What type and scale of resources should be necessary to achieve the goals set?

Selecting Suppliers

Conventional purchasing practice advocates dealing with a small number of suppliers, ideally single sources of supply since more than one source can be regarded as a waste of resources. In the case of buying services, a single sourcing strategy may be the only option. For example, it would not be possible to have a works canteen run by more than one service provider.

Long-term relationships with suppliers are important to encourage supplier loyalty and to help improve the service.

Evaluating Suppliers

Product buying emphasises the importance of product quality, supplier relationship and delivery performance.

The procurement of services should also focus on these aspects of performance, the quality of the service and service delivery.

Negotiation with Suppliers

With a product, a supplier would be awarded a contract on the basis that they that can provide a consistently high quality product with no incoming inspection, ensure punctual deliveries, work with the buyer to solve problems, and agree upon a fair price.

The contract award should be based on the service representing the best value for money. VFM means more than just price – it is the totality of the economic package.

Chapter Summary

Product buying has both differences and similarities with buying services.

Services tend to be done by people. The content of the work depends on their inputs and care for the customer (the purchaser).

Key stages in developing service contracts are:

☐ defining the requirement.

☐ selecting suppliers.

☐ evaluating suppliers.

☐ negotiating with suppliers.

10. Capital Goods Acquisition

Introduction

This chapter will examine the procurement of capital items, considering how this may differ from the procurement of stock items. It will also examine life cycle cost issues, payback calculations, compatibility issues (the importance of ensuring that capital items purchased are complementary to existing equipment), maintenance and training issues and after-sales support.

General

Definition of 'capital' equipment

'Items that are expected to produce benefit to the firm over a period longer than the accounting period in which the expenditure was secure'.

The following capital equipment characteristics help to create further under-standing of the nature of capital equipment, as well as how it differs from stock items.

☐   **High cost/single item** – capital items tend (although not always) to be high cost and to be single, often unique, items.

☐   **Depreciation** – it is usual for a company's accountants to depreciate the item over its projected life span. This is done to represent the reducing value of the item over time.

☐ **Financed from capital** – if the item is purchased outright, it will be paid for out of the company's capital fund. There are alternatives to outright purchase that will be considered later

☐ **Tax considerations** – these differ from country to country but, usually, there are tax advantages for a company purchasing a piece of capital equipment.

☐ **Loans and grants** – there may be loans/grants available from either central or local government for the purchase of capital equipment. This may be particularly true if the equipment is seen to contribute in some way towards the re-generation of an area.

☐ **Postponable** – the decision to purchase may be capable of being postponed until (e.g.) a more favourable time period.

☐ **Consequential decisions (sales and labour)** – there may be other decisions consequential to the procurement of a piece of capital equipment. An example would be the need to take on more labour to operate a new piece of equipment.

☐ **Adapted terms and conditions** – the company's normal terms and conditions of purchase are not normally adequate to cover capital procurement. It may, therefore, be necessary to add/subtract some terms or even develop a complete set of new terms for capital purchases. An example would be the negotiation of a guarantee, which is normal for capital purchases but not so for stock item procurement.

☐ **Problems of specification** – specifications are often much more complex for capital equipment than for stock items. Often performance specifications need to be used to try to incorporate suppliers' expertise to generate a 'bespoke' piece of equipment.

Examples of Capital Equipment

Source: C. K. Lysons 'Purchasing and Supply Chain Management' Prentice Hall.

☐ **Buildings**.

☐ **Installation equipment** – used directly to produce the goods and services. Examples include plant and machinery. Different types of plant and machinery will be used in different industries but specific examples would include drilling rigs and platforms in the oil production industry.

☐ **Accessory equipment** – used to facilitate the production of goods/services. This is durable, major equipment used to support the production of goods and/or services. Examples include large turbines, compressors, heavy-duty cranes and materials handling equipment. Installation and accessory equipment often coincide, but there is an important distinction best explained by means of an example. An aeroplane purchased by an airline would be 'installation equipment' whereas the same aeroplane purchased by an oil production company to facilitate the movement of personnel would be 'accessory equipment'.

☐ **Operating equipment** – semi-durable minor equipment that is moveable, used to support the production of goods and services. Examples might include safety equipment and special footwear.

☐ **Tools and instruments** – semi-durable or durable portable minor equipment associated with the production of goods and services. Examples include computers (PCs), timing devices, tools such as drilling bits.

☐ **Furnishings and fittings** – all items needed to fit buildings for their organisational purpose. Examples include carpets, furniture, shelves, counters and benches.

Committee approach

In many organisations a capital procurement committee is set up to consider all capital purchases. The purpose of this is to involve all departments in the organisation that may be concerned with the purchase of the equipment to consider such aspects as:

☐ specifications.

☐ the need to bring in potential suppliers to discuss specifications (performance specs).

☐ terms and conditions of contract.

☐ life cycle cost/investment appraisal issues.

The role of the procurement function in this process should be:

☐ to ensure that commercial issues are considered alongside technical ones. In many companies, decisions as to capital procurement are made almost exclusively on technical grounds.

While it is important to remember that, ultimately, the equipment must be capable of performing the function for which it is being purchased, commercial issues should be brought into play as well. This prioritising of technical issues may cause the procurement function to take a 'back seat' in such purchases.

☐ to negotiate the contract with the chosen supplier. Even if technical issues have been uppermost in terms of source selection, the buyer should be charged with the contract negotiation. This, after all, is a procurement skill.

Food for thought

Consider a recent capital purchase in your organisation. What was the role of the procurement function?

Alternative methods of acquisition

As indicated above, outright purchase of capital equipment is not the only means of its acquisition, there exist also the possibilities of leasing and contract hire. The actual decision depends on such issues as:

☐ whether these alternatives exist in the company's environment - not all countries have such sophisticated lease/hire alternatives as others.

☐ what the company actually wants the equipment for.

☐ how long the company needs the equipment for.

☐ whether capital is available.

The following table should help to summarise the relative advantages and disadvantages of the three means of capital acquisition.

	Buying	Leasing	Contract Hire
Advantages	Capital asset Low cost Ownership Resale Depreciation	Releases capital Tax + VAT Balloon schemes Profit/asset ratio Buyback	Full service Flexible Seasonal New technology Match demand/supply
Disadvantages	Capital tied up Running costs Profit/asset ratio Disposal	Costly No asset Contract terms inflexible	Costly No asset Contract

Buying used equipment

One alternative method of acquiring many types of capital equipment is to buy used items. Used equipment may be purchased from dealers' auctions or direct from previous owners. Thriving 'used' markets exist in many countries for the following types of equipment:

- ☐ Vehicles.

- ☐ Materials handling equipment.

- ☐ Storage equipment (racking, etc.).

- ☐ Office equipment such as photocopiers/computers.

Advantages of buying used equipment

- ☐ The cost is usually lower than that of new equipment (often substantially so).

- ☐ Used equipment may be more readily available, although this does depend on the nature of the specific equipment and the state of the 'used' market in the particular country.

- ☐ Used equipment may have a long life and be protected by guarantees. This is especially true if the equipment has been re-built or re-conditioned.

□   Investment appraisal and life-cycle costing techniques can be used to ascertain the economic viability of a 'used' purchase. Often, it may be more economically viable over the long-term to buy 'used' and it can, sometimes, be economically viable to buy 'used' but not to buy 'new'.

□   A used machine may be more compatible with existing ones in the organisation, thus reducing the cost of carrying spares. This comment depends on the nature of the equipment to be purchased and on that of the existing equipment in the organisation.

□   It may be possible to inspect the equipment in use under actual operating conditions. This is a very useful possibility but does depend, again, on the type of equipment.

Avoiding pitfalls in the procurement of 'used' equipment

The most obvious pitfall here, indeed the one that would put many buyers off buying 'used', is the possibility that, due to its previous use, the equipment may not be reliable or may not have a long life-span.

In the UK, laws such as the Sale of Goods Act and Trades Descriptions Act (see chapter 14) afford some protection to the buyer of used equipment and many other countries will have similar legislation. However, it is always best when considering the procurement of used equipment to adopt the principle of *caveat emptor* (let the buyer beware) and take as many precautions as possible over the quality and reliability of used equipment under consideration.

Such precautions might include the following.

□   Ask the vendor whether a history of the equipment is available and study it in conjunction with technical personnel if it is.

□   Is there any indication of the age of the equipment? Examples might be a serial number that could be checked against manufacturer's records or a certificate of manufacture/ registration.

□   Try to ascertain how well the equipment has been maintained during its previous working life. The assistance of technical staff to inspect the equipment from this standpoint may be required, and the buyer could ask the vendor if any records of maintenance exist. If so, these may be studied. This is essentially the equivalent of the service history that should be available for a used car.

☐ Ascertain whether spares are available and, if they are, for how long this situation will continue. Used equipment is more likely than new equipment to require spares and, for this reason, this point is very important.

☐ Compare the cost of the used equipment with that of the new. Does it represent good value?

☐ Is the vendor well-established and enjoying a good reputation? The buyer should avoid at all costs buying equipment from a 'fly-by-night' operator.

☐ Consider the general and special terms and conditions, if any, that might apply to the purchase. Do any of them cause particular problems?

☐ Is the vendor attempting to supersede any statutory protection available to the buyer with a guarantee? If so, this should set off 'alarm bells' for the buyer.

☐ Ascertain whether the vendor will allow any trials or test/approval period for the equipment. This can be the best way of ensuring that used equipment is of suitable quality and reliability.

☐ Ascertain whether the vendor will allow inspection by an independent assessor (such as SGS[1]). If the buyer is not allowed to test the equipment or is not able to carry out a full inspection personally/in conjunction with technical personnel, this may be a good substitute to ascertain the equipment's quality/reliability.

☐ Ascertain the cost of dismantling, transporting and re-assembling/ installing the equipment. These 'extras' may make the used purchase prohibitive when compared to a 'new' purchase.

☐ Ascertain whether the equipment has been rebuilt or reconditioned. Rebuilding is a more comprehensive process than reconditioning, and rebuilt machines will usually sell for between 50% and 70% of the price of similar new equipment whereas reconditioned items will usually sell for between 40% and 50% of the price of a new item.

Develop an action plan for the procurement of a piece of used equipment, paying particular attention to how to avoid pitfalls such as those mentioned above.

[1] Société Générale de Surveillance, a Swiss company specialising in third party inspection

Life Cycle Cost Issues

Life cycle costing is sometimes known as 'terotechnology' and is one of a number of methods of carrying out investment appraisal relating to the prospective acquisition of capital equipment. Investment appraisal may be defined as, 'Appraising the economic soundness of the investment in capital equipment over its life span.'

Investment Analysis

- Method.

- Payback.

- Rate of return.

- DCF.

- Life cycle costing (Terotechnology).

Definition

'Terotechnology is a combination of management, financial, engineering and other practices applied to physical assets in pursuit of economic life-cycle costs.'

To explain further, terotechnology involves:

- The selection and provision of permanent (ie. non-consumable) physical resources used in the production and services.

- caring for those resources effectively and efficiently.

- co-ordinating them to help achieve overall minimum costs over their life cycle.

- feeding back information to improve them.

Life cycle costing may be described as the establishment of the total cost of acquisition of equipment when performing its function throughout its operational life and may include:

- original price.

- appraisal studies.

- research and development.

☐ operational costs.

☐ maintenance costs.

☐ training and other support costs.

☐ de-commissioning and disposal costs.

All these, relative to each piece of equipment under consideration, must be forecast at the outset. In this way, when the buying company is considering purchasing equipment from one of a number of potential suppliers, life cycle costing may be used to identify the 'best' purchase.

If life cycle costs are presented as a graph it usually looks something like the following:

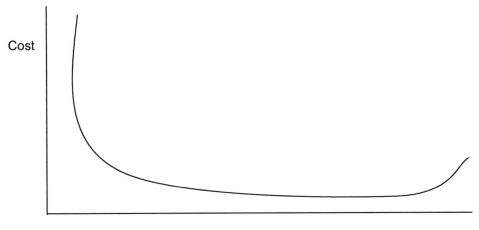

The two things to note from this graph are:

☐ The high cost at the outset representing the capital outlay. If the item were leased or acquired on contract hire, there would be no such initial cost.

☐ The curve goes up towards the end of the life cycle, showing the increased maintenance costs as the equipment becomes older and the cost of disposal.

In order to make life cycle costing work effectively, factual and quantitative information must be sought, evaluated and eventually input to analysis. Suppliers' optimistic claims must be challenged. This may be facilitated by visiting fellow buyers' sites in which installed equipment currently operates. It should be possible to develop a checklist of questions that the buyer can use as a means of determining the life cycle cost of alternative selections.

Payback Calculations

Payback is one of the simplest methods of carrying out investment appraisal. Its purpose is to show which one, out of a range of prospective proposals, will pay for itself the quickest and begin to generate profit for the organisation. The use of Payback, as with other investment appraisal techniques, involves forecasting cash flows, both positive and negative, that will accrue to the organisation because they have invested in the equipment. Payback may be expressed as follows:

Payback = $\dfrac{\text{Net investment (£s) NI}}{\text{Annual operating saving (£s) AOS}}$

It should be noted that:

- net investment includes tax allowances/liability and annual depreciation.

- AOS is used on the assumption that each proposal will generate a saving or contribute to the organisation's profitability.

While Payback is the simplest method of investment appraisal it does have some major weaknesses:

- The preferred investment is the one that pays for itself the quickest, not necessarily the one that gives the best return over its lifetime.

- It assumes that income received from an asset in the future has the same value as current income.

- It fails to take into account the total cost of ownership of the asset.

The following example should illustrate both the advantages and weaknesses of Payback: (*Source of example: C. K. Lysons – 'Purchasing and Supply Chain Management' Prentice Hall*)

An organisation is considering buying one of two machines each costing £20,000. The net cash flows after operating costs and expenses, but not allowing for depreciation, are forecast to be as follows:

Year	Cash Flow Machine A (£)	Cash Flow Machine B (£)
1	5,000	4,500
2	5,000	4,500
3	5,000	4,500
4	5,000	4,500
5	5,000	4,500
6	-	4,500
7	-	4,500
	25,000	31,500

Payback   –   machine A $\dfrac{£20,000}{5,000}$ =   4 years

           –   machine B $\dfrac{£20,000}{4,500}$ =   4.4 years

Machine A has the better payback but machine B's return extends over two further years.

Rate of return

This involves trying to assess the average annual net profit after depreciation and other cash outlays as a percentage of the original cost. Three calculations are required:

The annual rate of depreciation: Cost – $\dfrac{\text{Residual value}}{\text{Estimated value}}$

Using the example under 'Payback' seen earlier, assuming each machine has a forecast residual value of £1,000, annual depreciation rates would be:

Machine A   = $\dfrac{£20,000 - £1,000}{5}$ =   £3,800

Machine B   = $\dfrac{£20,000 - £1,000}{7}$ =   £2,174

Subtract depreciation from the average annual profit:

Machine A   =   £5000 – £3,800   =   £1,200

Machine B $\quad = \quad$ £4,500 – £2,174 $\quad = \quad$ £1,786

Express net annual profit after depreciation as a percentage of the initial cost:

Machine A $\quad = \quad \dfrac{£1,200 \times 100}{£20,000} \quad = \quad$ 6%

Machine B $\quad = \quad \dfrac{£1,786 \times 100}{£20,000} \quad = \quad$ 8.93%

On this basis, Machine B is the most profitable.

Discounted cash flow (DCF)

Discounting shows the value at the present time (present value) of a sum of money receivable in the future and is the reverse of compounding. The present value may be calculated by dividing the amount of money, currently held, by that to which it would have grown at a given rate of compound interest. Thus, £100 invested now at 10% interest would be worth £110 in one year's time. On this basis, £100 received in one year's time would currently be worth:

$$\frac{£100}{£110} = 0.9091$$

This figure is then multiplied by itself to give the current value of £100 received in two year's time: 0.9091 x 0.9091 = 0.8264.

For each year into the future the previous year's figure is multiplied by 0.9091 (assuming an interest rate of 10%). Thus, year 3 is 0.8264 x 0.9091 = 0.7513, and so on. In practice, published tables provide the annual figures.

Using the net present value (NPV) method, the minimum required rate of return on the investment is determined. This is a management decision. The present value of forecast future cash flows is discounted at this rate. If the sum of these cash flows is greater than the initial expenditure the investment will give a higher return than forecast. Using the examples of machine A and machine B seen earlier and a minimum required return rate of 10%, DCF for both machines would be as shown in the table.

Machine A has a total return less than the initial investment of £20,000 whereas machine B's return exceeds the original figure. Therefore, machine B would be the better investment.

DCF may also be used for comparing whether it would be better to invest in a piece of equipment or to invest the equivalent amount of money in the bank or building society. In the example above, assuming a 10% rate of interest from the bank, it would be better to invest £20 000 in the bank than to buy machine A but the reverse is true for machine B.

Year	Cash Return (£)	10% Factor (£)	NPV (£)
Machine A			
1	5,000	0.909	4,545
2	5,000	0.826	4,130
3	5,000	0.751	3,755
4	5,000	0.863	3,415
5	5,000	0.621	3,105
6	-	-	-
7	-	-	-
	25,000	-	18,950

Year	Cash Return (£)	10% Factor (£)	NPV (£)
Machine B			
1	4,500	0.909	4,090
2	4,500	0.826	3,717
3	4,500	0.751	3,380
4	4,500	0.683	3,073
5	4,500	0.621	2,795
6	4,500	0.565	2,542
7	4,500	0.513	2,309
	31,500		21,906

Compatibility Issues

Where a piece of capital equipment is being purchased to combine with other equipment already in the possession of the buyer's company, great care should be taken to ensure that the new equipment will be compatible with that already existing.

If the new equipment is to be supplied by the same supplier who provided the existing equipment there is less likelihood of a problem in this regard than if a new supplier is to be used.

Whether or not a new supplier is to be used, it is good practice to request that all potential suppliers visit the buyer's premises to investigate the equipment currently in use. It should also be made a condition of tendering that all tenderers submit a guarantee that their equipment will be compatible with the buyer's existing equipment.

Food for thought

Have there been any instances in your organisation where equipment has been purchased that is not totally compatible with existing equipment? If so, why was this, do you think? How was the situation resolved?

Maintenance and Training Issues

Maintenance

Pieces of capital equipment usually need maintenance during their working life. If the piece of equipment has been produced especially for the buyer's company ('bespoke') it is important to negotiate a maintenance agreement with the original supplier.

This may not be so important with pieces of equipment bought 'off the shelf' although the likelihood of this happening with (e.g.) pieces of plant is probably small in most organisations. In the case of 'off the shelf' equipment, the buyer's company may have its own engineers who would be qualified to undertake maintenance or the buyer may wish to investigate the possibility of sub-contracting this work.

For bespoke pieces of equipment it is important to forecast:

☐   the nature and extent of maintenance required.

☐   the frequency of routine maintenance such as services.

☐   the projected cost of such maintenance.

☐   the availability and cost of any spare parts that may be required to support maintenance. The period of time for which the supplier will undertake to make spares available is very important. The longer the spares availability period, the longer the buyer's company is likely to be able to use the equipment.

These forecast costs may be included in any of the calculations already examined to ascertain which of a range of proposals is likely to be the 'best' one.

Training

If a new piece of equipment is to be purchased, the buyer's company's staff may need training to be able to operate the equipment properly so as to get the best use out of it, as well as to avoid damaging it through incorrect usage.

If the supplier is willing to undertake such training, the cost of it must be ascertained and included any kind of investment appraisal carried out. It is important to consider the possibility of re-training being necessary at some point in the future. If this is likely, its forecast cost must, again, be included in any investment appraisal.

If the supplier recommends training for the buyer's workforce, such recommendation needs to be taken seriously. It is possible that the supplier might be trying to gain money under false pretences but, on the other hand, evaluation of the recommendation may show that the training would be extremely valuable. Certainly, it would not be worth possibly wrecking an expensive piece of equipment for the sake of some training, even if it does appear expensive.

It could be worth investigating training agencies other than that provided by the supplier. Care should be taken, however, because non-approved training may invalidate any guarantee offered by the supplier. Lack of training, where recommended by the supplier, might also invalidate the guarantee.

Food for thought

What steps does your organisation take to ensure that staff are trained to use new equipment? How are costs calculated and included in any investment appraisal carried out?

After-Sales Service

The provision of spares was referred to earlier and this is an essential aspect of the negotiation for the purchase of capital equipment, as is the provision of an adequate level of after-sales service. Where the item is 'standard', the buyer should ensure, by negotiation with the supplier, that spares will be readily available from the supplier's stock.

If the equipment is 'bespoke', the buyer should try to negotiate a period of spares' availability after the equipment has been commissioned. A period of 10 years would be a useful guideline. Additionally, it would be useful for the buyer to keep a set of drawings to enable the purchase of spares from elsewhere in the event of any problem with the original supplier.

The after-sales service required should be agreed at the negotiation stage and included as a term of the contract.

It is good practice, also, to agree a meaningful guarantee from the supplier so that there is a period of time to enable the buyer's organisation to identify problems. These should then be rectified at the supplier's expense during the guarantee period. It should be noted that, in return for a meaningful guarantee, the supplier may seek to impose restrictions on the manner in which the equipment is operated such as a limit on the number of hours per week of operation. The extent to which these are accepted, or otherwise, is a matter for negotiation between the parties.

International issues

If a piece of capital equipment is purchased from overseas, the following issues relating to after-sales service and general 'back-up' need careful consideration:

      □   **Availability of spares** – this has been considered, in general terms, but can be more problematic when the supplier is based overseas. Does the supplier have infrastructure in the buyer's country so that spares will be readily available to the buyer? If spares need to be shipped especially, long delays with the equipment out of commission are likely.

      □   **Domestic agent** – is there a supplier's agent in the buyer's country who will be able to expedite problems such as breakdowns? Having someone close at hand to turn to in the event of problems is, at least, reassuring.

      □   **Manuals in translation** – are manuals that have been translated properly into the language of the buyer's country in existence? The use of such manuals will alleviate many problems. Unfortunately, poorly translated manuals are, at best, of little use and, at worst, dangerous, so care should be taken with these. The provision of good manuals by the supplier should be made a term of the contract.

Food for thought

Do you ever purchase capital equipment from overseas? What special steps, if any, do you take to avoid problems such as those alluded to above?

Chapter Summary

In this chapter, the general nature of the purchase of capital equipment has been considered, including:

- The role of the buyer in the acquisition of capital items.

- The different approaches to the acquisition of capital equipment, such as outright purchase, leasing and contract hire.

- The different approaches to investment appraisal such as:
  - Life cycle costing
  - Average rate of return
  - Payback
  - Discounted cash flow

including the relative advantages and disadvantages of each method.

- The need for equipment purchased to be compatible with the buyer's company's existing equipment.

- The need for buyers to ensure that negotiation takes place with the supplier to ensure the provision of maintenance and after-sales service, as well as consideration of the cost of such provision.

- The need for training of the buyer's company's staff to accompany the purchase of capital equipment and associated costs.

Case Study

Eastland Foods

Eastland Engineering Ltd. is rapidly expanding. The products produced by the company are selling very well. The Board is seriously considering an expansion into European markets and this would entail an expansion of the delivery fleet. The vans currently used would be unsuitable for cross-channel journeys.

Accordingly, John Smith has been asked to investigate the best way of obtaining a new refrigerated lorry. In particular, the Board has asked John to consider leasing and contract hire options as funds are currently limited and any European expansion would involve a heavy marketing cost, thus depleting available reserves.

John holds initial discussions with the Finance Director who tells him that no funds can be made available from the capital reserves for any new vehicles. However, the overdraft facility with the company's Bankers could be used, but the rate of interest charged would be 12% per annum.

The Finance Director suggests leasing as an alternative to purchase and John confirms that he is investigating this possibility.

After discussions with several dealers, John narrows down his options and is faced with three alternatives:

1. Outright Purchase

The desired lorry can be bought outright for £28,000 but John estimates a resale value of £5,000 after five years. Regular servicing would obviously be needed and from his knowledge of this he anticipates annual services costing:

End of Year	Service Cost
1	£1,000
2	£1,500
3	£1,500
4	£2,000

2. Finance Lease

The lorry can be obtained with finance provided by a leasing company. The cost would be £5,000 per year payable annually in advance. The lease period would be five years. Service costs would be borne by the user and would be as (1) above.

3. Contract Hire

This option is offered by a Main Dealer. The hire period would be five years, and includes four annual services to the required standard. Payments are to be made monthly and are fixed at £550 per month.

While considering these options, John Smith is informed that the Board have now decided to proceed with the planned expansion, and that approval in principle has been granted for the acquisition of a new lorry. John is required to put to the Board a proposal for the most economical way of proceeding.

Task

If you were John Smith, which of the three alternatives would you recommend, and why?

11.   Ethics and Ethical Issues

Definition

'Ethics is concerned with the moral principles and values which govern our beliefs, actions and decisions.'

Business ethics have been described as:

'The systematic study of moral (ethical) matters pertaining to business, industry or related activities, institutions or practices, and beliefs can also refer to actual standards, values or practices of beliefs.'

Both definitions from:

> *C. K. Lysons, ('Purchasing and Supply Chain management' Prentice Hall)*

Examples of unethical behaviour might include the following:

☐   Cash payments.

☐   Gifts.

☐   Lavish hospitality.

- Misuse of company assets.

- Conducting private activities at work.

- Inflated expense claims.

- Favouritism towards particular suppliers.

- Stationery/PC consumables.

- Unauthorised issues from stock.

- Inappropriate use of company staff.

There is much emphasis, so far, on the 'moral' aspect of ethics. While this is very important, many people would take the view that there are good, practical, reasons why it is important for procurement staff to behave ethically. The general 'thrust' of most published codes of ethics is that buyers should not allow anything to impair impartiality. In other words, buyers are charged with spending their organisation's money and should do so in a way that is totally impartial.

Contracts should be awarded to suppliers because the supplier represents the best value for money not because the buyer is favouring that supplier for whatever reason.

If any buyer believes that impairment of impartiality 'does not matter', it should be remembered that, in extreme cases, if contracts are awarded to suppliers for reasons other than 'best value', the misspending of company money could lead to bankruptcy. This would leave the buyer jobless. Is it better, in the long-term, to receive 'bribes'/'gifts', etc. or to have a job?

It would be useful to consider some of the practical issues surrounding unethical practices using the list of examples above.

Cash payments

If a supplier were to make a payment to a buyer in return for the award of a contract this would be illegal in many countries, being classed as bribery, and may render the buyer subject to criminal proceedings. In many organisations, at the very least, such an arrangement would be construed as gross misconduct and would be punishable by instant dismissal.

Whatever the legal situation, a buyer in receipt of cash payments from a supplier is going to do his/her best to award as many contracts as possible to that supplier.

Gifts

The giving of gifts by suppliers to buyers is a common practice in many countries. In the UK the giving of a bottle of whisky at Christmas is quite common, for example. It is often said that such gifts are merely a way of 'saying thank you' for past business and should not be regarded as a 'softener' for future business.

Perhaps not but, when gifts become much larger and more valuable than a bottle of whisky, it is pertinent to ask whether the supplier is giving the gift for the benefit of its corporate health or whether it expects to receive something tangible, such as a large contract, in return. If contracts are awarded to suppliers because the buyer knows that he/she will continue to receive gifts from the supplier the buyer's company's money is not being spent impartially.

Hospitality

To a great extent, comments made under 'gifts' apply here. Many people take the view that the occasional lunch with a supplier is harmless. In many countries, however, there is a huge 'corporate hospitality' business specialising in arranging for companies to take corporate clients to (e.g.) major sporting events, theatre, etc. In 1993 some £36m was spent on corporate hospitality in the UK alone. Companies spending the large amounts of money on such events are not doing it 'to be nice'; they expect some kind of return, usually in the form of the award of contracts.

Misuse of company assets

This refers to the general misspending of company money or using company assets for the buyer's personal benefit. Any such activity means that the buyer is not focusing on the job at hand and is not likely to be spending company money wisely and impartially.

Conducting private activities at work

The occasional private telephone call, perhaps in emergency, is common practice and not really what is being referred to here. What is being described is the spending of a large percentage of the buyer's time carrying on such activities as (e.g.) running private businesses or running clubs of some kind.

Not only is this time-consuming but also probably involves the use (misuse?) of company resources such as telephones, computers, etc. Again, this kind of activity means that the buyer is not focusing on the job at hand and is likely to be carrying out professional activities in a hurried and, therefore, unprofessional manner.

Inflated expense claims

Unfortunately, a fairly common occurrence and one that, in cases of highly inflated claims, is often construed as gross misconduct and renders the culprit liable to instant dismissal. People who believe that such activities are 'par for the course' or 'nothing to worry about' should remember that they are, in fact, fraud. Any fraud is likely to render precarious the company's ability to survive and prosper in the long-term.

Favouritism toward particular suppliers

This may because of gifts and/or hospitality (see above) but is also possible because a supplier's company is owned by, or managed by, a close friend or relative or because the buyer has invested in shares in the company. None of these situations is remotely illegal but, if they lead to contracts being awarded in appropriately, are dangerous for reasons already stated. The advice of many published codes of ethics, in such situations, is that the buyer should declare the interest they have to their superior so that the situation is 'open'. The superior may then make a decision as to how to proceed.

Stationery/pc consumables

This refers to the common practice of 'removing' (e.g.) pens/pencils, floppy disks, etc. These items do not have a high intrinsic value and many people take the view that such activity is harmless, sometimes described as a 'perk'. It should be remembered, however, that if everyone carried out such activity, all the time, a large number of company assets would disappear. Again, this could mean that the future of the company is precarious.

Unauthorised issues from stock

Often such things as small tools are taken and, again, this is common practice in some organisations. The comments above under 'Stationery' apply.

Inappropriate use of company staff

This covers such activities as persuading company staff to do private jobs either on company premises or 'at home'. Again, this represents a drain on company resources and a lack of focus on the job at hand, with the same potential, harmful, consequences for the future of the company. What determines the degree to which people/organisations adhere to ethical codes?

This often stems from the commercial culture of the organisation. Additionally, much may arise from the personal standards of the head of procurement. A head of procurement who behaves impeccably him/herself and makes it known that he/she expects similar standards of behaviour will usually find that staff follow the lead.

Much depends on the concept of being 'professional'. In this respect, the following guide would be useful:

> **Food for thought**
>
> Is there an organisational perspective of ethics in your organisation? If so, what is it?

Ethics – concept of 'professional'

Precepts

☐　　Integrity.

☐　　Competence.

☐　　Resources.

☐　　Law.

In terms of organisations, much depends on directives arising at the highest level. It is often the case that public bodies have much higher standards of behaviour and tighter controls on such behaviour than private companies, although not exclusively so.

The usual reason for this is that such organisations are spending public money and have to account for that expenditure extremely rigorously.

Combating unethical practices

The following are useful guidelines in this respect:

☐　　**Effective supplier selection** – being seen to have good systems for supplier selection including clear, open, tendering procedures with assessment and award criteria clearly laid out in the Request for Proposal (RFP). Refusing to deal with suppliers who offer gifts, etc. obviously and lavishly and who make it clear they will do 'anything necessary' to gain a contract is also good practice.

☐ **Competent and professional staff** – ensure that staff are properly selected to fill positions and that they are trained, either in-house or externally, to the highest standards. Guidelines and guidance should be regularly provided so that staff know what is expected of them.

☐ **Contract performance** – suppliers should be rated (either as part of a formal vendor rating scheme or informally) based on their performance of contracts and the manner in which they fulfil them not on ethically questionable issues.

☐ **Directives (EU)** – these only apply to public sector organisations and private companies providing public services/utilities in countries that are EU members. However, the EU directives that give guidance on ethical matters are useful and their guiding principles may be adopted by any organisation.

☐ **Well-paid staff** – it should be obvious that, if staff are well paid, there will be less likelihood of unethical behaviour, because staff will be in less need of gifts/cash payments and will be less ready to jeopardise their job and career prospects through unethical behaviour.

Implementing an ethical code

The following steps would be considered useful in terms of implementing a workable ethical code that staff and management would support, and which should go some way towards combating unethical behaviour.

Source: Chartered Institute of Purchasing and Supply Study Guide: Introduction to Supply and Materials Management.

☐ Decide on what is 'acceptable' – as has already been considered this may depend on culture/organisation, etc.

☐ Write down a code of ethics – so that staff know what is expected.

☐ Sell the benefits of the code and the sanctions that go with it – so that everyone inside and outside the organisation is aware that the code exists and what is likely to happen to staff who flout it.

☐ Ensure senior management supports it – without management backing it is not likely to be successful.

☐ Publicise it to suppliers, internal clients, buyers and management – so that everyone involved is aware of it and its provisions.

- Put it into action – this will involve training and support and an initial amnesty for those who have 'done wrong' in the past.

- Monitor outcomes.

Food for thought

What steps are taken to combat unethical behaviour in your organisation?

Finally, in this section, what evidence may there be of ethical behaviour by buyers?

This evidence may be considered as follows.

Declaration of interest

Any personal interest that may affect a buyer's impartiality in any matter relevant to his/her duties should be declared. This relates to (e.g.) suppliers being owned or managed by friends or relatives. In such a case, the buyer should inform his/her superior and allow that person to make a decision as to the way forward. It could be that the superior would:

- leave dealings with the supplier to the buyer's professionalism and discretion or arrange for another buyer to deal with that supplier.

- insist that the supplier be removed from the approved supplier list.

This last one is somewhat extreme, however, and buyers should beware of rejecting good suppliers because of connections between them and members of staff of the buying organisation.

Accuracy/confidentiality

The confidentiality of information received in the course of duty should be respected and should never be used for personal gain. For example, news that a supplier is doing well might lead the buyer to invest in shares of that company. There is nothing intrinsically wrong with this, but it should be remembered that possession of shares might lead the buyer to award to the supplier more and more contracts which may be inappropriate, to boost chances of a good dividend.

Competition

The nature and length of contracts and business relationships with suppliers can vary according to circumstances. These should always be constructed to ensure deliverables and benefits. The buyer is not prevented from entering into long-term relationships with suppliers providing these will deliver measurable benefits. Buyers should use their discretion as to how frequently tendering should be used for the re-award of contracts.

Gifts

A common policy here is that business gifts, other than items of a very small intrinsic value such as business diaries or calendars, should not be accepted. Where the refusal of gifts may cause offence, the following are possible methods of dealing with them without causing offence or jeopardising the buyer's ethical stance:

- ☐ accept the gifts and place them in a 'pool' to be shared out equally later.

- ☐ accept the gifts and raffle them off between all staff.

- ☐ accept the gifts and donate them to charity.

Hospitality

The buyer should not allow him/herself to be influenced or perceived by others to have been influenced in making a business decision as a consequence of accepting hospitality. The frequency and scale of hospitality accepted should be managed openly and with care, and should not be greater than the buyer's employer is able to reciprocate.

Many people recognise that good business may be carried out over lunch, etc. The problem is to stop such activity being perceived as the supplier's 'treat'. To this end, some organisations provide buyers with expense accounts so that the buyer can pay for hospitality in turn with the supplier.

Food for thought

Are you aware of any relationships with either suppliers or customers that might be harmed by unethical behaviour?

Chapter Summary

In this chapter the subject of ethics and ethical behaviour has been examined, including:

☐　　General ethical issues such as the meaning of 'ethics' and examples of unethical behaviour.

☐　　Why it is considered important to behave ethically and the types of behaviour that would be encouraged, including cultural differences.

☐　　The main points that might be included in a formal code of ethics.

☐　　The impact that unethical behaviour may have on total costs.

☐　　The potential damage to relationships with both suppliers and customers arising from unethical behaviour by the buyer.

Case Study

Tom and Harry

Tom Peg is the Contract Manager for the Lysons Manufacturing Company based in Western Europe. The company has had a successful history since its formation in 1970. Tom is responsible for all the purchasing and supply of packaging materials. He has a staff of some 20 people including a Stock Controller and a Stores Manager. Tom feels that he has the purchasing side of his job well covered. He has managed to develop two very good suppliers over the years. These two companies supply almost 80% of the company's packaging materials.

One of the suppliers (the larger of the two) is represented by Harry Kelpful. Purely by chance, Tom and Harry were at college together in the 1950's. The two had lost contact over the years, but had now re-established their friendship via their relationship at Lysons. For many years the two have worked closely together. Harry was able to help out on several occasions with technical support that was very useful to Tom and his company. The two men played golf together at college and soon took up the sport again. They played together once a month at the start, but this soon became a weekly date. The majority of the games were played at Tom's club. The membership fees for Tom's club were quite expensive and so Harry usually picked up bill for lunch and drinks after each game.

Recently, the reject rate of some of the packaging supplied by Harry's company began to increase. The Production Manager for Lysons became very concerned and wrote a short memo to Tom. Tom called Harry to discuss the issue of poor quality. During the discussion it became clear that Harry was under a great deal of pressure. It seems that the company have recently adopted a new production process and that it was not running as it should. Harry was very worried that the company would lose its customers, and he would soon be out of a job. Tom decided that Harry had been such a good supplier in the past that he was worth protecting in the short term.

Tom: "I'll write a memo to the Production Manager telling him to look to his own operatives for the root of the problem."

Harry: "What help will that be Tom?"

Tom: "I should give you a few weeks to get your production problems sorted out!"

Harry: "Yes, I see what you mean."

Harry is very relieved that he has this breathing space.

Harry: "Listen Tom, why don't you let me pay for your club membership this year?"

Tom: "Well er ... "

Harry: "After all I use your club almost as much as you do, it's only right I should pay!"

Tasks

1. Do you feel the relationship between Tom and Harry is ethical?

2. Taking the role of the Managing Director of Lysons (who has come to find out what is going on) what would you do?

12. Performance Measures

Definition of Control

> 'Control is the continuous comparison of actual results with those planned, both in total for separate sub-divisions and taking management action to correct adverse variances or to exploit favourable variances.'

The control function of management rounds off the total process of managing the human, material and financial resources of an organisation. Its primary aim is to measure performance against standards with a view to enabling corrective action to be taken to keep plans on course. Controlling activities are closely linked to planning and decision-making activities.

Strategic, Administrative and Operational Control

Control should take place at three levels – the strategic level, the administrative level and the operational control level. Control must influence the behaviour of individuals and groups towards the implementation of the corporate strategy and towards progressive change.

There are six useful guidelines:

      ☐   Distinguish between control at different levels in the management hierarchy. When managers take control action, they ought to be aware of what they are trying to achieve. Is their control measure intended to have an immediate impact (e.g. 'firefighting' at an operational control or budgetary level)? Or will it take time for the measure to have a tangible effect because it is for longer-term strategic benefits?

☐ Individual managers should be identified as having the responsibility for certain matters, and authority to take control measures. At a budget level, responsibility centres should be established for accounting purposes and budgetary control reporting.

These responsibility centres might be revenue centres, costs centres, profit centres or investment centres. In other words, there must be an organisation structure for control.

☐ The key performace indicators (KPI) for control should be identified. Managers responsible for taking control action must be informed about what the key factors are and why they are critical.

☐ Control reporting should be timed sensibly. Depending on the level of control (strategic, budgetary, or operational), control reports should vary from the occasional to regular and frequent.

☐ Suitable targets and standards should be applied. For example, it might be reasonable to set profit targets for all the products in a company's product range, but well-established, thriving products ('cash cows') ought to have a different profit target from new products. Targets should be tailored to suit individual circumstances, and control applied accordingly.

☐ Control reports should contain relevant information and should not contain unnecessary details about irrelevant items. A production report, for example, should not include unnecessary details about sales volumes and deliveries, and selling costs, because these will be of no interest to the production manager receiving the report.

However, some sales details might be relevant if production delays are affecting sales levels and profits.

Control Process

The control process involves a series of actions that follow in sequence (see figure 1).

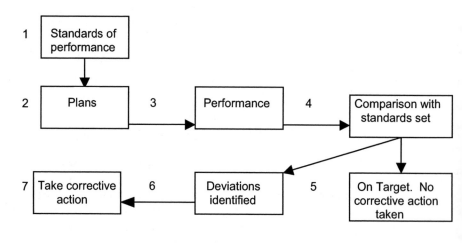

Figure 1

This process of control includes three main underlying components:

- Setting targets or standards which serve as guidelines for performance.

- The measurement and evaluation of actual performance.

- Corrective action where it is needed in the form of a control decision.

Setting targets or standards

Targets and standards of performance stem from a decision about what the objectives of the organisation should be. The overall objectives adopted in the planning process serve as a foundation for all subsidiary quantified targets. From divisional and departmental targets to the performance standards for every echelon of manager and employee in the organisation.

The purpose of setting targets or standards is to in the materials department is to:

- Tell the materials manager what he/ she must accomplish, and ensure they are given the authority to make appropriate decisions.

☐ Indicate to the materials manager how well his or her actual results measure up against the targets, so that he/she can take control action where needed.

Corrective action

Before taking corrective action, it is important to determine the apparent reason for any unsatisfactory performance, and whether the reason is one which will lend itself to control action or whether it is an uncontrollable matter. For example, when production levels are low and rejects high, attempting to improve the quantity and quality of output by increasing supervision may only increase labour costs, if the real reason for low performance is poor quality inputs from suppliers or unclear specification from the customer.

Strategic Procurement Performance

Figure 2 indicates how the criteria by which procurement operations were measured and therefore controlled over the past 40 years have changed significantly and this corresponds with changes in the needs and attributes of the people who resource procurement operations today.

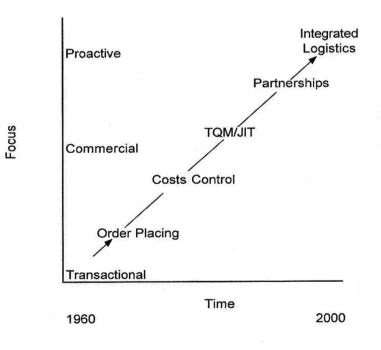

Figure 2

Benchmarking

'Benchmarking may be defined as the systematic and continuous search for best practices that will lead to superior performance. It is a very structured activity involving the careful selection of bench marking partners'.

This is the process of comparing the performance of individual materials operations with similar operations in similar (or different) organisations. This stems from the need to compare our performance against others and will provide hard evidence of effectiveness. The problem of many internal systems of control is that they can be designed to give the results required or expected rather than the actual results. The Centre for Advanced Purchasing Studies (USA) undertook a benchmark study for the petroleum industry in the USA, (see Major Conclusions).

It should be noted that there are no legal problems with collecting such data, since it is related to the purchasing department's methods and non-pricing practices.

Best Practice Groups

Another technique used to establish meaningful measures of performance is the formation of best practice groups. These are formed to enable the participating organisations to share their best practices with group members and, in return, to expose the methods and processes of fellow participants. This often provides insights into improvements and alternative methods of achieving objectives that had currently not been recognised. A good example of a Best Practice group is that facilitated by DPSS Consultants and involves many leading organisations.

Control Criteria

A key issue in the materials management control process is that of deciding what needs to be measured to give an accurate picture of performance. To some extent this is contingent on the organisation and the materials involved. However, the fundamentals must include the total cost of ownership; this has been defined as:

'The cost of manufacturing an item or supplying the labour/component of a service is embraced to a greater or lesser extent in the contractual price. The cost of acquisition, however, begins with in-house design and specification and ends with delivery to the user. The cost of installing, operating, maintaining and finally decommissioning are all associated with the life span of these items or services. The three components of price, acquisition activity cost and life cycle cost represent the total cost of ownership'.

TOTAL COST OF = PRICE + ACQUISITION + LIFE CYCLE
OWNERSHIP   COST   COST

Therefore, control systems should focus on the elements that make up the TCO.

Measuring the Effectiveness of Materials Management in Supply Chains

There are a number of established methods available to the materials manager to enable him/her to be able to control the business process, via the measurement of performance and thus indicating the degree of control and highlighting the areas that need corrective action. These methods include the following:

Budget Controls

'Budgeting is a systematic translation of operating plans for each materials unit into financial terms including the resource allocation decisions associated therewith'.

Budgeting as a control process

Probably the most widely accepted function of the budgeting process is control. But at the outset it should be noted that the budget does not control; people control. The control aspect of budgeting demands that sufficient planning and co-ordination have already been accomplished. Only then is it time for control action on the part of managers.

Adherence to a plan must be achieved in an environment composed of a delicate balance between motivation and constraint. The budget should not stunt enthusiasm and creativity, but by the same token it should not let developing problems or windfall successes occur without encouraging the organisation to adjust to these events in a fashion which yield improved utilisation of resources. Control is accomplished by having responsible individuals review periodically the operational aspects and results of their units' activities. An efficient system of information gathering must be instituted and utilised.

A caveat is in order here, insofar as the information system and frequency of communications are concerned. Remember that the budgeting system is an overhead. It consists of information generated over and above basic legal reporting requirements. The benefits of this additional information must be more than would have been experienced without the additional information. The budget always should remain the instrument of the planning control process and not become the end in itself.

Types of Materials Budgets

    ☐   Operating (including staff).

    ☐   Capital.

    ☐   Consumables.

Advantages of the Budgeting Control System

Budgeting is the most popular form of materials control. This is because it has many of the features of a generically effective control system, including:

    ☐   Economic.

    ☐   Appropriate.

    ☐   Timely.

    ☐   Reaches the right person.

Ratio Analysis

A number of ratios have been developed to assist the materials manager to identify particular aspects of the process that may need to be more rigorously controlled and more importantly compared with previous years and those of competitors.
The following ratios are among the most common:

Key Ratios

$$\frac{\text{Operating cost}}{\text{Total purchases}} \quad \text{x} \quad 100 \quad = \quad \text{Overheads}$$

$$\frac{\text{Operating costs}}{\text{Total orders}} \quad \text{x} \quad 100 \quad = \quad \text{Cost per order}$$

$$\frac{\text{Total value of purchases}}{\text{Turnover}} \quad \text{x} \quad 100 \quad = \quad \text{Materials inputs}$$

$$\frac{\text{Total value of orders}}{\text{Number of buyers}} \quad = \quad \text{Buyer productivity}$$

$$\frac{\text{Value of purchases}}{\text{Number of orders}} \quad = \quad \text{Value per order}$$

Key Perfomance Indicators (KPI)

There are many key indicators that can be used by management to provide useful data and focus for the control process. These include:

- Stock turn.

- Average value per order.

- Stock investment levels.

- Number of new suppliers sourced.

For indicators to be effective, a clear idea of the value of an indicator is essential.

The following questions should be asked of each indicator:

- What purpose does it serve?

- Does it tell the purchasing and supply director what he/she wishes to know?

- How accurate or reliable an index is it?

- Is there a more suitable index which could be used instead?

- Which other indices need to be looked at in relation to this index?

Profit Centre Analysis

This method regards the materials department as a part of the undertaking that controls assets and is responsible not only for expenditure but also for income. The materials executive is therefore expected to base his or her decisions on profit criteria, and his/her performance is measured by the profits generated by the department, (see example of value of assets controlled by the materials manager).

To reach the expected return of 15 per cent other than by increasing the notional profit, the supplies department will either have to reduce the investment in inventory or the operating expenses.

Advantages of Profit Centre Approach

- Provides a measure of the efficiency of the materials function.

- Allows the materials manager to control his/her budget and spend to save money.

- Increases the status of the materials function by providing measurable objectives.

Example $

Inventory   1,500,000

Materials department
floorspace and equipment   250,000

Stores floorspace and equipment   750,000
                                     2,500,000

Annual rate of return required
by the undertaking on assets
employed   15%   =   375,000

Estimated annual operating expenses

Materials   150,000

Stores   475,000   625,000

Total expenses and return (a)   1,000,000

Total purchases for year (b)   20,000,000

(a) divided by (b) =   5%

Transfer cost of supplies to user departments will therefore
be 5% + a notional supplies profit (say 1%)   =   106

Therefore profit on turnover of £20,000 = 20,000

Return of assets controlled by supplies = $\dfrac{\$200,000 \times 100}{2,500,000}$ = 8%

Controlling Activities and People

Fundamentally, we can divide the measurement of performance and control process into two parts. These are controlling activities (what people do) and the people themselves (how they perform).

Activities

How much of the activities of the materials department are undertaken is a function of direction and methods?

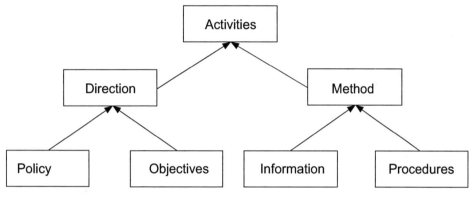

Figure 3

These in turn are functions of organisation, policy and objectives; the information provided to staff and the procedures they have to follow.

People

How well people perform these activities is a function of their credibility and expertise.

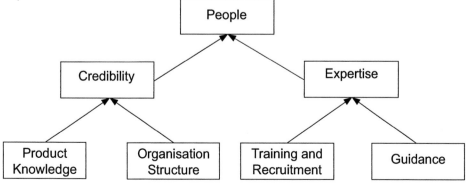

Figure 4

These, in turn, are functions of their degree of product knowledge and the organisation position of materials. Their individual expertise is a function of their training and their recruitment. The degree of guidance provided by senior managers is also crucial.

Chapter Summary

☐ Control is a process that sets targets and measures performance against these targets.

☐ Controls do not constitute control.

☐ Budgeting is the most popular of control systems.

☐ Systems tend to control people or activities.

☐ Ratio analysis, Profit centre analysis and comparisons are useful control systems.

☐ Benchmarking is becoming a very effective means of comparing the performance of one organisation with another.

Case Study

PTM Ltd

PTM Ltd is a large multi-national chemical manufacturer. The company has plants in Europe, USA and the Far East. Head of Procurement, Peter Jackson, feels that the function could perform much better and that improvement opportunities are being missed because of a lack of information regarding the performance of procurement.

At a recent meeting with the Head of Finance, Peter is told that from a budgetary point of view the procurement function is well on target for the current year. However reports from the customer indicate a high degree of dissatisfaction with the service provided by procurement. and indeed the strategic management of the business do not feel procurement is really adding value.

Task

Identify the tangible and intangible activities of both a strategic and operational nature that need to be measured, to enable Peter Jackson to be able to demonstrate the true performance of his department.

13. Internal Customer and External Supplier Relationships

Introduction

This chapter will examine internal customer relationships including work teams, communications with suppliers including '360 degree' feedback, the need to be open and ethical in dealings with suppliers, development of an initial understanding, by suppliers, of buyers' requirements and the need for clear and fair terms and conditions of contract.

Internal Customer Relationships

There is increasing emphasis on the notion of the 'internal customer'. A 'customer' is whomever the buyer (or any other staff member) is providing a service to, and an internal customer might be the next stage in the supply process or the requisitioning department.

A two-way relationship is required here because, whilst it is important for the buyer to provide the right service to users, the buyer can only do this if provided with the right information with which to work in the first place.

The general 'message' is that, if everyone, at every stage of the process attempts to 'delight' their customer, together, the whole supply chain will 'get it right' and delight the end customer. 'Delighting the customer' is exceeding the customer's expectations.

Interfaces with internal customers

It has been commented that it is of no use the procurement function forging strong links with suppliers if its own interface with internal functions is poor. Typical functions that procurement may interface with are:

- **Sales** – it is important to obtain advance warning of (e.g.) sales promotions, so that Procurement can purchase the items required to support such activities.

- **Operations** – in any organisation, most of the items purchased by procurement will be required by Operations. It is important that procurement receive accurate and timely information relating to requirements, if they are to stand any chance of satisfying or delighting them. In turn, Procurement needs to ensure that the best service level possible is provided to Operations.

- **Finance** – Procurement and Finance will need to collaborate over issues such as invoice payment and credit ratings of potential suppliers.

It is important that the interface with each of these areas is well-developed and effective. Poor communication can lead to wasted time and resources, and delay the supply of goods or services to the end customer. The growth of world-class concepts (e.g. Total Quality Management) has led to a need to improve interfaces between internal functions. This improvement should lead to business being able to respond more quickly and accurately to changing customer demands and a rapidly changing environment.

An improvement in the nature of interfaces might be brought about by:

- meetings between different functional areas.

- improvement in general communications.

- development of integrated databases.

- more cross-functional teamwork, such as:
  - supplier development – involving procurement, finance, engineering and operations
  - cost reduction – all areas
  - supply chain improvements – all areas

- greater involvement by procurement in all aspects of the business.

Communication and the Nature of Relationships

There is a great deal of emphasis today on the development of strategic relationships with suppliers. The view is that, in the past, relationships were 'arm's length' or even adversarial. These approaches are still found today, but many buyers strongly believe that the development of closer, more collaborative relationships with suppliers yield many advantages to both parties.

This collaborative approach is sometimes known as 'Partnership Sourcing'.

Definition of Partnership Sourcing

'Commitment by both customers and suppliers, regardless of size, to a long-term relationship based on clear, mutually-agreed objectives to strive for world-class capability and competitiveness.'

The nature of the 'partnership' approach and more 'traditional' approaches may be summarised as shown below.

Traditional	Commercial / Partnership
Arm's length	Close
Adversarial	Co-operative
Negotiating price	Co-managing costs
Limited contract	Broad involvement
Problem solving	Prevention
Incoming inspection	Process control
Gate keeper	Facilitator
Contract-based	Trust and performance
Short term	Long term
Win/lose	Win/win

It can be seen already that the partnership or 'commercial' approach emphasises communication at all stages of the buying/selling process. Examples of the need to communicate include the following:

    □   **Co-managing costs** – both parties involved in working together to reduce costs, rather than the more traditional approach of trying to persuade the supplier to reduce prices.

- **Broad involvement** – both parties involved at all levels to try to ensure that each gains from the partnership. This may involve such concepts as Early Supplier Involvement (ESI), Total Quality Management (TQM), etc.

- **Prevention** – both parties working together to prevent quality problems rather than trying to solve problems after they have occurred.

- **Win/win** – the emphasis is on both parties winning from the arrangement. The nature of what might constitute 'winning' will be considered below.

The nature of 'win/win'

The win/win approach refers to the idea that both buyer and supplier gain advantages from the arrangement between them. The term 'win/win' is often used in connection with negotiation. This is important because negotiation, a process of communication, is often seen as the focal point of the partnership approach.

Advantages to the buyer

Buyers increasingly require greater levels of service and support from suppliers than used to be the case. Increasingly, buyers require:

- contribution from suppliers at the design stage such as ESI and Value Engineering.

- commitment from the supplier to manage quality over time and to improve quality.

- commitment from the supplier to examine the reduction of costs proactively.

- commitment from the supplier to develop products technologically over time on a proactive basis.

It is a commonly held belief that suppliers will not give the kind of commitment levels outlined above if relationships are adversarial and short-term.

Advantages to the supplier

These might be summarised as follows:

- Long-term business/security.

- ☐   Profit margins.

- ☐   Ethical relationship/treatment.

- ☐   Prompt payment.

- ☐   Satisfying work.

- ☐   Opportunities for expansion.

- ☐   Enhanced reputation.

There are a number of issues here in terms of adversarial relationships. For example, under an adversarial relationship, late payment and the forced reduction of profit margins were commonplace. Note should also be taken of the 'long-term' aspects of the partnership approach.

The promise of business from the buyer over the long-term will usually be a great motivating factor for suppliers. Obviously, this promise will only be brought to fruition if the supplier continues to satisfy (or even 'delight') the buyer.

Strategic procurement

Consideration of partnerships has taken procurement into a strategic area and it would be useful to consider the nature of strategic procurement and contrast this with the more operational role traditionally held by procurement.

Operational	Strategic
Transactional	Value added
Short term	Long term
Focus on cost	Focus on customer
Internal view	External
Operational focus	Strategic focus
Performance statistics	Benchmarking processes
Procedures and systems	Results
Technical process	Business process
Efficiency	Effectiveness
Transactional	Added value
Ratio	Benchmarks
Re-active	Pro-active
Operational	Strategic

Choice of appropriate relationship

Buyers may sometimes develop the impression that partnership relationships should be entered into with all suppliers all the time. This, however, is not the case. A variety of relationships are possible and buyers need to be aware of the range and situations in which each type of relationship would be suitable.

Definitions of an effective relationship for supply

1. **Master/servant relationship** – focuses on achieving one party's objective, generally with the customer as the master and the supplier as the servant.

2. **Master/butler relationship** – similar to the above but acknowledges that to be fully effective, the parties must work together.

3. **Fair trading relationship** – this relationship will be driven by the exchange of value and acknowledges the two-way element which enables a relationship top become truly effective.

4. **Harmonious relationship** – a relationship in which the parties exhibit trust, openness and commitment and adherence to a clearly defined agreement.

5. **Reciprocal/symbiotic relationship** – parties deliberately work in co-operation with each other to achieve known goals.

6. **Ethereal relationship** – parties have mutual business objectives and work together to achieve these.

The question then arises as to what type of relationship the buyer should aim to have with a supplier in each situation. A useful model to help make this decision is the **Kraljic matrix**.

This categorises all purchases (thus including services as well as tangible items) according to two parameters: buyer attractiveness and supply market strength.

□　　　**Buyer attractiveness** usually arises from the buyer's spend or potential spend, but can arise from issues such as whether the buyer's company is considered a 'prestige' customer.

□　　　**Supply market strength** usually arises from how many suppliers there are in the supply market. Many suppliers gives each individual supplier low strength and few suppliers gives each individual high strength.

The matrix operates as follows:

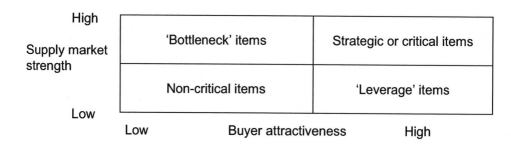

Figure 1

Each category will now be examined in turn

- ☐ **'Bottleneck' items** – here the buyer, typically, has a low spend and there are few suppliers. This means that the buyer is dependent on the supplier or even 'begging for crumbs from the supplier's table'. This can be highly problematic, and a useful suggestion would be for the buyer to work with internal personnel (users, technical, etc.) to try to alter the specification so that the purchase would be in another category. Failing that, the best approach is to try to cultivate good relationships with suppliers of this category of item. Consolidating similar purchases onto one supplier can give the buyer more leverage than would otherwise be possible.

- ☐ **Strategic or critical items** – here, there will typically be few suppliers, but the buyer will have a high spend. Thus, the business will be important to both parties. The buyer should look to form strategic alliances and think of partnerships that focus on long-term pro-activity and mutual benefit.

- ☐ **Non-critical items** – here, spend will be low and there will be many suppliers competing for business. In this situation, buyers do not want to spend time dealing unnecessarily with low-value items, and the best approach is to 'automate these purchases as much as possible' and encourage such scheduling practices as 'direct requisitioning'.

- ☐ **'Leverage' items** – here, typically, there are few suppliers but the buyer has a large spend. This means that the business is very attractive for suppliers, and the power rests with the buyer. It is here that the buyer can maximise the contribution to the 'bottom line' and profitability by using commercial power and the competition that exists in the supply market to obtain the 'best' deal. The buyer may change supplier as often as is necessary when buying this category of item.

Food for thought

Think about some of your purchases. What category on the Kraljic matrix would you place them in? What scope is there for changing your approach with any of the purchases based on what you now know of 'targeting' relationships?

Development of supplier partnerships

Generally, supplier partnerships are developed when a supplier base has been rationalised. Many buyers have undertaken a process of supplier base rationalisation in recent years, because many advantages are perceived to arise from buying from fewer suppliers and working more closely with the suppliers that remain.

Here are steps towards this.

Rationalising the supplier base

There are six steps involved:

☐ Identify where purchased items are currently bought and where they could be bought.

☐ Determine the important criteria for selecting suppliers.

☐ Evaluate current suppliers.

☐ Select the best supplier for each product based on the evaluation.

☐ Where suppliers do not achieve an acceptable level of performance, evaluate potential suppliers.

☐ Select the supplier base.

If the buyer then wishes to develop a partnership-type relationship with a supplier, the following process has been suggested by Partnership Sourcing Limited, a company co-formed by the UK Confederation of British Industry and the Department of Trade and Industry:

1. **Understand your needs**

   ☐ Identify your strategy for partnership sourcing (the suppliers of your products and the markets that you sell to).

2. **Sell the idea**

   ☐ Sell the idea to your senior management that a long-term, stable and continuously improving supplier base is a source of competitive advantage.

   ☐ Sell the concept to the rest of the organisation.

   ☐ Sell the concept to potential partners (customers and suppliers).

3. **Audit the supplier base**

   ☐ Identify the major suppliers that can contribute to the success of your organisation.

   ☐ Define the criteria for selecting partners.

   ☐ Assess the attitude of the supplier's senior management towards working in partnership.

   ☐ Audit and understand the strategies of the suppliers and their future direction.

4. **Define the style of the relationship**

   ☐ Agree the style and content of the partnership relationship.

   ☐ Agree the objectives of the relationship.

   ☐ Agree the areas of the joint relationship that need to be improved and the areas for continual improvement activities.

5. Make the partnership work

☐ Advise everyone involved in the process.

☐ Start work to build the environment for 'partnering'.

☐ Agree the monitoring and measuring systems.

☐ Build and develop the relationship.

☐ Continuously monitor progress against the measures.

☐ Revisit the measurement system to set new targets.

It should be seen that there is much emphasis on setting criteria to judge the effectiveness of partnerships and on monitoring progress against these criteria. After some time has passed the buyer should audit the success and areas of failure in the partnership and evaluate the possible future extension of the programme to cover other suppliers.

Food for thought

Can you think of any suppliers that you currently use where you could develop partnerships? What specific advantages would you expect to gain from such a course of action? Would you approach the development of any such partnerships in the way outlined above? If not, what differences would there be and why?

'360-Degree' Feedback

There is much emphasis, when considering supplier partnerships, on mutual benefit. The purpose of '360-degree' feedback is to ensure that both buyer and supplier derive mutual benefit from the arrangement.

'360-degree' feedback is where the buyer assesses the supplier's performance and the supplier assesses the buyer's. In this way, obstructions that were caused by either party to the performance of the relationship can be identified and mutually resolved.

Food for thought

What do you understand by 'buyer's performance'? How may aspects of buyer's performance hinder a relationship?

Information may be exchanged between buyer and supplier in face-to-face discussion or by the use of questionnaires. Once again, the emphasis here is on communication.

A 360-degree feedback approach should be based on:

☐ Shared mutual objectives and compatible benefits for both parties.

☐ Agreed problem solving methods.

☐ Shared risks according to who can best manage them.

☐ An active search for continuous measurable improvements.

☐ A way of managing the relationship proactively.

Advantages to the buyer

☐ The elimination of waste at the interface between buyer and supplier.

☐ Improved quality and delivery.

☐ Shortened lead times.

☐ Enables unnecessary cost to be 'designed out' of products.

☐ Improves the security of supply.

☐ An increase in procurement's contribution to the profitability of the organisation on a continuous basis.

Advantages to the supplier

☐ Market advantage

□   Improved technological capability

□   Improved financial stability and the ability to plan resources over the long-term.

□   Better payment arrangements.

□   Opportunities to improve management capability.

In order to obtain the kind of mutual benefits outlined above, it is often considered necessary to adopt a cross-functional approach to the assessment. This would enable such issues as design and logistics to be considered and improved, as well as traditional commercial aspects of the relationship.

It should be borne in mind that buyers may create problems for suppliers. For example, if performance measurements identify that the supplier is not meeting delivery targets, a cross-functional team might find that late delivery is the result of poor planning and scheduling by the buyer's company.

'Open and Ethical'

The importance for buyers to operate in an ethical fashion at all times is well documented, and is supported by ethical codes published by such organisations as IFPMM and Chartered Institute of Purchasing and Supply (UK).

Many people think that such codes and other ethical guidelines focus only on gifts, hospitality and out-and-out corruption. However, the ground rules that lie behind these codes require a fundamental pursuit of:

□   Honesty.

□   Accuracy.

□   Confidentiality.

If these are missing for any reason, it is difficult to develop a meaningful collaborative relationship. For example, the knowing exaggeration of a sales requirement, during preliminary discussions with a supplier, only to reveal a much lower requirement when the price and other terms are agreed, is contrary to most ethical codes.

Many buyers do not appear to see any harm in over-indulging in hospitality, accepting the occasional gift or telling 'white (?) lies' about (e.g.) future requirements. However, for a relationship to prosper, a fundamental underlying 'bedrock' of truth and honesty is required. Otherwise, each meeting between buyer and supplier will become an adversarial negotiation in which each will keep certain information from the other to use for bargaining purposes at the right time.

Within any relationship there is always likely to be some tension surrounding the perceived self-interest of each party. However, the relationship will only grow when both parties perceive that their best self-interest lies in sharing the overriding benefits that come from unity. This is often known as the 'open-book' approach.

Open-book approach

This is the full and open sharing of cost information between buyer and supplier. In some environments, such information has been traditionally seen as being 'sensitive' and not to be shared. However, there are many benefits to be gained, by both parties, from the sharing of such information.

Essentially, the 'open-book' approach allows both parties to be aware of each other's costs and cost drivers. This can allow, for example:

- the buyer to suggest alternative raw material suppliers for the supplier to use to reduce raw material costs.

- the supplier to be reassured that the buyer's company is not making excessive profits out of the supplier's cost reduction initiatives.

- inefficiencies in both operations to be identified and rectified.

Food for thought

Do you have any suppliers that you would be prepared to use the 'open-book' approach with? What benefits do you think both parties would gain?

Clear and Fair Terms and Conditions

Most buyers will be familiar with terms and conditions of contract (the 'small print'). The terms for complex, high-value contracts may run to many pages. However, when dealing with collaborative relationships, it should be realised that the contract terms are no substitute for the necessary attention to the initial supplier selection.

No contract in the world will enable a supplier to do something they were incapable of doing before the contract was agreed.

Some people believe that the detailed development of complex terms and conditions, designed to support one party's interests at the expense of the other's, is wasteful and inimical to good supplier relationships. Such people believe that, if a relationship based on trust is the ultimate goal of both parties, something more akin to a framework agreement is all that is necessary.

The idea of this is that the mutual willingness to make the relationship work will, effectively, remove the need for a detailed contract. The argument that follows this is that terms should be clear and not be designed to be misleading. The following analysis would be useful here.

Standard	Framework Agreement	Open/ Memorandum
Lack of trust Transactional Master/servant Relationships Short-term	Some trust Flexibility Commercial Mid-term	Trust Mutuality Risk and rewards Long-term
Lack of incentives Penalties/damages Strict terms/conditions	Penalties/incentives Prescription plus match supply and demand	Incentives Focus on solution Output spec. Demand-pull
Blame Prescription Procedure	Matches supply and demand	Working together
Adversarial	**Co-operative**	**Partnership**

This move towards a 'framework agreement' or even the less formal 'open or memorandum' type of agreement is mirrored by the means of dispute resolution being available. It should always be remembered that, no matter how collaborative a relationship, problems may occur at some point, and some thought to their resolution is necessary.

Chapter Summary

This chapter has examined the nature of internal relationships, and the development of collaborative buyer/supplier relationships with emphasis on the means by which these may be developed. It has also examined:

◻   The role of communication at all stages of agreements with suppliers.

◻   The need for and uses of '360-degree' assessment and feedback, so that both parties may assess each other's performance and any weaknesses identified may be corrected.

◻   The need for clear and fair (i.e. not misleading) terms and conditions of contract.

Food for thought

What scope exists in your organisation for reducing the extent and complexity of terms and conditions? Would this approach work with some suppliers but not others?

Case Study

MKL Limited

MKL is a large international company based in the Netherlands. The company, which has operations in Europe and the Far East, has a long history of profit and product excellence. The strategy in the past has been one of integration, and the business has acquired many related businesses over the past 10 years, including a distribution company. The company's main activity is the production of a wide range of packaged foods.

The responsibility for the supply of all MRO and consumables rests with the Central Procurement Group (CPG). The supply of these materials is cause for much concern throughout the group. Many plants complain of excessive inventories and yet a lack of critical materials. Costs, in relation to the acquisition of materials and services, continue to rise, quality is suspect and many of the relationships that MKL have with its suppliers is based upon an adversarial approach.

Contractors often complain of a lack of information and yet demands for JIT service. Distribution is a major problem, given that the Head of the Business reports to the Marketing Director. The supply chain for many MRO and consumables is long and complex, lead times are often counted in months and the reputation of CPG throughout the group is pretty low. The procurement process is very transactional and the majority of contracts are awarded on the basis of lowest price.

The company has a policy of keeping its suppliers on their metal by competition and often playing one against the other. Very little in the way of information about requirements is communicated to suppliers, the process works on a need to know basis.

The Head of Procurement believes that if the company tells the supplier what is required they will just boldly state they can do it! Suppliers and contractors are forced to hold considerable inventory just in case MKL make a sudden demand for product, as they often do. This annoys the suppliers as they know large product promotions are planned months in advance. It seems to the suppliers that MKL do not understand about the complex processes involved in producing the materials they require.

Task

What improvements would you suggest to help overcome the problems outlined?

14. Introduction to Legal Issues

Introduction

At this stage, it would be useful to introduce you to an area of study that some people find involved and difficult, although it must be emphasised that the intention here is merely to provide an overview of English law as it applies to procurement and in particular to everyday purchasing and supply situations.

You should note that law is potentially a huge subject area to study, and here we will do little more than 'scratch the surface'. Our studies will be focused on law as it applies to contract formation, and the subsequent performance and completion of contracts. The specific aspects of law that we will examine are:

- An overview of the English legal system.

- Contract formation.

- Terms and conditions of contract including the 'battle of the forms'.

- Legislation that is relevant to contracts and other procurement situations.

- The obligations of both buyer an seller in contracts

- Dispute resolution.

- Vitiating factors (factors that might render contracts void or 'voidable').

- Remedies available to the buyer for breach of contract by the seller.

- Liquidated damages and 'penalties'.

Why do buyers need to study law?

Many people, both practising buyers and CIPS students, make the point that there is no need for buyers to study law for the following reasons:

- A large percentage of situations which could end in litigation (i.e. be taken to court) are settled by negotiation between the parties without recourse to law.

- If you do need to take someone to court, you consult an expert (a solicitor or the company's legal department).

Both of these statements are true, but in the small percentage of situations which negotiation cannot settle, you need recourse to the law, and if you know nothing of the law how do you know whether you need to consult an expert? Without some knowledge of the law the following situations might happen:

- you might allow a situation to develop to a point where consulting an expert is too late to protect your interests.

- without some knowledge of the law you might not fully understand what the expert tells you.

- Finally, if your first course of action is to try to settle an issue by negotiation, and if you know that the legal position of both parties is favourable to you, you can negotiate from a position of strength.

The English Legal System

We will start with a very brief examination of the English legal system. The purpose of this is to distinguish civil law from criminal law – it is civil law with which we are mostly concerned here. You should note that we are only concerned with English law. There is no such thing as 'British' law because Scotland has a separate legal system which differs from the English system in a number of important aspects. If you are reading this as part of your CIPS studies it might be useful to know that you can opt to be examined, in any subject that concerns law, under Scottish law.

The two main parts of the legal system are criminal law and civil law.

Criminal law

This covers such crimes as murder, theft and road traffic offences. It also covers a few offences which have to do with purchasing transactions, such as breaches of the Trade Descriptions Acts (1968 and 1972) which make it an offence to give a false trade description of goods or a false indication of price in the course of business or trade.

Persons charged with offences under criminal law are called defendants. The person bringing the action is called the prosecutor. If defendants are found guilty they are punished by the court, usually by fines or imprisonment.

Civil law

Criminal law is not concerned with punishment but with compensation. It includes contract law and the Sale of Goods Act, as well as other pieces of legislation, which we will examine later, that affect purchasing and contracts such as the Unfair Contract Terms Act. Actions are usually brought by the aggrieved party, called the plaintiff (not the prosecutor), who sues (not prosecutes) the defendant.

A plaintiff who wins the case will be compensated by the court in some way, usually by a sum of money to be paid by the defendant, known as damages although other remedies are possible and we will examine some of these later.

How do laws come into existence?

In Britain and in some other countries, there are two main sources. Sources of law include both statutes and common law. Countries which have law known as 'common law' are known as 'common law countries'.

Statutes become law by Act of Parliament. Common law, on the other hand, is assumed to exist already and to be known to everyone. This assumption was perhaps appropriate to an earlier time when there were fewer people living in smaller communities and in a more traditional culture. It now seems artificial, and it could be said that common law consists of (rather than being evidenced by) the decisions of judges in cases under the common law. Case law and judge-made law are phrases which stress this aspect of common law. It is worth noting that judges exist to interpret and enforce law, not to invent it, but new common law is being developed constantly.

An example of this is the law covering negligence, which, according to Richard Jennings, writing in 'Supply Management' magazine of 3 March 2005, "...was developed from nothing over the past century by judges with virtually no help from parliament". This view can be linked to the fact that the decisions of judges also affect statute law. Very few statutes are written so clearly that it is easy to understand them and, in fact, some are written so obscurely that it is very difficult to understand them. This might appear to be a somewhat bizarre state of affairs, but the reason for the arcane, sometimes convoluted, language used in law is that any particular law attempts to cover every possible, or at least foreseeable, situation that might involve that particular Act of Parliament.

Consequently a number of court cases have been about what phrases and sentences in particular Acts of Parliament mean, and how provisions of an Act are to be interpreted.

A non-purchasing example of this is the case fought a few years ago whereby a woman named Diane Blood was fighting for the right to be impregnated using her dead husband's sperm, this course of action apparently being against the law. The judge in the case was quoted in the media as saying that it was 'his job to interpret' what Parliament had in its collective mind when it passed the law. Ms Blood won the case. In general terms, the findings of the court are regarded as part of the law.

Also, circumstances change, technology and commerce develop and questions arise as to how existing Acts apply in new conditions. If these questions are argued out in the law courts, the answers defined by the judges may also become part of the law.

Statute law thus comprises all those Acts of Parliament currently in force, plus the case law which clarifies the meaning or the application of the Acts. Also, some statutes enable government departments to make regulations which have the same force as the enabling statute.

Common law provides the context for statute law. For instance, it states what a contract is. It also includes laws which are not explicitly stated in writing in the way that statutes are, but nevertheless are evidenced clearly enough by case law.

As a member of the European Union, the UK is also bound by the Treaty of Rome most public sector organisations to advertise all purchasing requirements exceeding a variable sum, which at the time of writing (summer 2005), is the equivalent in Euros of about £100 000 (although this amount changes frequently) in the Official Journal of the European Union (OJEU); and to place contracts so as to obtain the best value for money and without discrimination on the basis of country of origin.

The Purpose of a Contract

A contract is a legally enforceable agreement between two parties: no more, no less. There is a common usage of the term 'contract' which refers to a type of order which covers the supply of an item on numerous occasions e.g. in a 12 month period. ('We have got pump ref. XYZ on contract'). This is an easily understandable but incorrect usage of the term. A better term for this kind of arrangement would be 'standing order' (or 'blanket order') and it is not what we will consider here.

As stated earlier, a contract is a legally enforceable agreement between two parties. It may cover the provision of goods or services by one party (the seller) in return for some kind of reward from the other party (the buyer). This 'reward' is usually money ('the price'), but the law does not stipulate that it has to be money, merely something 'of value'.

The basic purpose of a contract is to confer rights and duties on both parties to a contract in respect of the subject of the contract, 'the subject' being the product or service being bought and sold. In other words, a contract sets out formally the way in which the contract will be performed and the way in which the performer will receive reward from the other party, and the rights of either party in the event of the other party not doing what is required of them. For example, in a contract for the sale of goods, the contract will provide rules for the way in which the seller supplies the goods and the way in which the buyer receives them and pays for them.

It will also provide a means of recompense for the buyer if the seller (e.g.) does not supply the right goods at the right time and for the seller if the buyer (e.g.) declines to accept the goods or refuses to pay for them.

In summary, contracts could be said to provide rules for the conduct of business and 'remedies' for the aggrieved party if the other party does not abide by the rules.

How Contracts are formed between Purchasers and Suppliers

In practice, a contract is formed when both parties decide that it should be. However, for a contract to be legally binding, a number of occurrences must take place. These are:

- Offer.

- Acceptance.

  - Offer and acceptance taken together and indicating that both parties understand the nature of the subject of the contract is usually known as 'agreement'. This is sometimes referred to as *'consensus ad idem'*, usually translated as 'an agreement on the same thing' or a meeting of the minds'.

- Intention to create legal relations.

- Capacity to contract.

◻   *'Consensus ad idem'*.

◻   Consideration.

These are generally known as the 'essential elements' of a contract and we will examine the nature of each and give examples of how each might occur in practice. These 'essential elements' are very important, because, if someone is sued for breach of contract, they can show that no contract ever existed because one or more of these 'essential elements' was missing, the action would fail because you cannot breach something that never existed in the first place. Remember:

◻   If any one of these 'essentials' is shown to be missing, there is no contract.

◻   This can work against your interest if you are suing a supplier, but could work in your favour if a supplier is suing your company.

◻   It is generally in your interests to ensure that a legally binding contract exists subject to your terms and conditions if possible, so that your commercial interests are looked after.

Let us now consider each of these 'essential elements'.

Offer

This can be in the form of an offer to buy or an offer to sell. In 'simple' (i.e. private) contracts this can be a person saying 'would you like to buy this widget for £5', which would be an offer to sell or 'I will give you £5 for that widget', which would be an offer to buy.

In commercial purchasing terms an offer is usually one of the following documents:

◻   A purchase order (an offer to buy when sent to a supplier without a preceding enquiry or quotation).

◻   A quotation, bid or tender from a supplier (an offer to sell). You should note that, as a general rule, only a quotation giving specific details of price, delivery, delivery quantities, etc., in other words a specific, detailed, response to a buyer's request for quotation, would constitute an offer. A fairly vague response, merely stating that the goods were available at a particular list price, would probably constitute an 'invitation to treat' (see below).

Note: an enquiry sent by a buyer to a potential supplier is known as an 'invitation to treat' and, as such, has no legal consequence whatsoever. The same principle applies to a telephone call to a potential supplier asking if they sell a certain item, suppliers' catalogues, the display of goods on supermarket shelves or in a shop window and advertisements.

To be valid an offer must conform to the following prerequisites:

- ☐ It must be communicated, so that the other party may accept or reject it.

- ☐ It must be definite in substance.

- ☐ It must be distinguished from an 'invitation to treat'.

Additionally, an offer may be communicated in any manner whatsoever, i.e. in writing, in words, or by conduct. There is no general requirement that an agreement must be in writing and an offer may be made to a particular person, to a group of persons, or to the whole world. The case of *Carlill vs Carbolic Smoke Ball Co (1893)* established this last point.

In this case, the defendants were manufacturers of a medicinal product called 'The Carbolic Smoke Ball'. They placed an advertisement in a newspaper stating that if anyone bought the product, used it correctly and still contracted the 'flu, they would pay the person £100. They also stated that, as a token of sincerity, they had deposited £1000 in the bank.

Mrs. Carlill bought the product, used it correctly and contracted 'flu and claimed her £100. The company refused to pay, saying that the advertisement was a mere advertising 'puff' (i.e. a statement to the world at large) and that a contract could not be made with the world at large.

The court of appeal held that an 'offer' could be made to the world at large, and that, therefore, Mrs. Carlill was entitled to the money.

Termination of an offer

An offer may be terminated in one of the following ways:

1. Revocation

An offeror, (the party making the offer), may withdraw an offer at any time before it has been accepted. The revocation must be communicated to the offeree (the party receiving the offer) before acceptance.

2. Lapse of time

This may occur through any of the following:

- Passage of time, i.e. at the end of a stipulated time or after a reasonable time.

- Death, as long as the offeree was aware of the death prior to acceptance.

- An express or implied condition.

3. Counter offer

A counter offer made by the offeree, in which a term of the original offer is altered, constitutes a counter offer and destroys the original offer; this principle being established in the case of *Hyde vs Wrench (1840)*.

Here, the defendant offered to sell some land to the plaintiff for £1000. Two days later, the plaintiff made a counter-offer of £950, which was refused by the defendant. Subsequently, the plaintiff contacted the defendant and agreed to purchase the land for £1000 and sought an order of specific performance (an order made by the court requiring the defendant to perform their contractual obligations according to the terms of the contract).

The court refused to grant such an order, finding that the offer to pay £950 was a counter offer that had permanently destroyed the original offer rendering it incapable of acceptance.

Two things are important with a counter-offer:

- When an offeree seeks to accept an offer while stipulating some amendment to a term of the offer, it is really a counter-offer, and not an acceptance.

- That an enquiry for further information is not a counter-offer and does not affect the continued existence of the offer. Therefore, traditionally, an acceptance must be a mirror-image of the offer.

4. Rejection

The offeree may reject the offer, after which it cannot be revived.

5. Failure of a precondition

If the offer is made subject to the offeree satisfying some precondition, and the offeree fails to do so, the offer will fail to take effect, as established by *Financings Ltd. vs Stimson (1962)*.

In this case, a customer intended to buy a car on a hire-purchase agreement and duly completed a hire-purchase proposal form. The car was subsequently stolen from the dealer's premises and badly damaged. The next day, the hire-purchase company purported to accept the offer.

The Court of Appeal held that there was no contract because there was a condition in the offer that the goods, on acceptance, would be in the same condition as at the time of the offer and as they clearly were not, the offer was incapable of acceptance.

Acceptance

This is the person to whom the offer was made saying 'yes' (or words to that effect). Acceptance can also be implied – no words spoken or written, but the person's conduct implying acceptance. In terms of commercial purchasing, acceptance is usually one of the following:

☐   Acknowledgement of the order.

☐   A purchase order sent to a supplier in response to a quotation.

Note: if either of these documents differs in any respect from the original document it is responding to, it is not acceptance but a 'counter-offer' which destroys the original offer and, for a legally-binding contract to exist, must be accepted in turn. An example of this occurrence might be an acknowledgement form returned by a supplier, but with the delivery date altered from '2 weeks' to '4 weeks'.

As we will see later, terms and conditions can play a part in this area. An acceptance is a final and unqualified assent to all the terms of the offer and has the following prerequisites:

☐   It must be made while the offer is still in force.

☐   It must be made by the offeree.

☐   It must exactly match the terms of the offer.

☐   It may be written, oral, or implied by conduct.

    □   Where the offer is made in alternative terms, the acceptance must make it clear to which set of terms it relates.

    •   A person cannot accept an offer of which they have no knowledge.

Intention to create legal relations

Both parties must intend to create legal relations. In other words, both parties must intend that there should be a legally binding contract. Most legal cases fought around this issue result from 'domestic disputes' (e.g. if your father promised to buy you a car as a reward for passing your exams and then did not, if you sued him for breach of contract, the court would almost certainly decide that there was never any intention to create legal relations).

Generally, we can take it that forwarding documents labelled 'Purchase Order' with terms and conditions on the reverse to a supplier and a supplier responding with a document labelled 'Acknowledgement', possibly also with terms and conditions on the reverse, will be deemed by a court as an intention by both parties to create legal relations.

Capacity to contract

Everyone over the age of 18 has capacity to contract for themselves unless they are minors (i.e. under the age of 18), drunk or under the influence of drugs or suffering mental disorder. When we are discussing commercial purchasing we need to consider two issues: **Contracts entered into on behalf of a company** and that of **corporate capacity**.

Dealing first with contracts entered into on behalf of a company, the question arises as to who has capacity to contract on behalf of the company for which they work. The answer to this question is, in some people's view, deeply unsatisfactory and is certainly prone to the criticism of being 'woolly'.

It is this: the only people with absolute capacity are the owner, partners, or board of directors. However, the position of capacity of employees is more difficult and is as follows. If the other party 'reasonably supposed' that you have capacity to contract on behalf of your company, you do in fact have that capacity. This is otherwise known as the principle of 'ostensible authority'. In practice, this supposition – 'reasonable' or otherwise – depends upon the individual's job title and/or job description so that:

    □   People with job titles such as 'buyer', 'purchasing manager', 'sales representative', etc. clearly will be 'reasonably supposed' to have capacity to contract on behalf of their employers.

□   Equally clearly, people with job titles such as 'filing clerk', 'lavatory attendant', etc. will not.

□   Problems arise with people whose job title is 'production manager', 'chief accountant' and the like. The apparent seniority of such job titles would lead many people to 'reasonably suppose' that those individuals have capacity to contract on behalf of their employers.

The case of *British Bank of the Middle East v Sun Life of Canada (UK) ltd. (1983)* established that the level of authority to enter into contracts (i.e. capacity) must be consistent with normal practice in the industry and appropriate to the level of executive concerned.

The case involved a bank, relying on the authority of an assurance company's local manager, after enquiry and written assurance to commit the life office to a class of property transaction unusual in the procedures of life assurance companies, other than at head office level.

On appeal to the House of Lords, it was held that the written assurances given were not binding because they were issued by senior local management but not from the assurance company's head office even though the bank had written to the head office on two occasions.

Note: the above is one of the best arguments for ensuring that authority to purchase is centralised on the purchasing department. If a junior person makes a contract the company could probably get out of it by claiming that the person did not have capacity. If a senior or senior-sounding person makes a contract, it is far less likely that the claim of lack of capacity will work. Unfortunately, many senior people do not have the training or experience to ensure that the company's contractual interests are looked after, whereas purchasing staff should.

Over the years unscrupulous stationery sellers have used this principle to work a 'scam'. It works like this: seller contacts a junior person or a secretary and ascertains that they have some responsibility for buying stationery. Seller confuses this person by using technical terms ('ream', 'quire', et al) and convinces them to buy a 'sample' quantity.

Unfortunately the 'sample' quantity turns out to be five years' supply.

When the buying company tries to rescind (get out of) the contract by saying that the individual concerned does not have capacity to enter into contracts for such large amounts of money, the seller says that he/she 'reasonably supposed' that they did (after all, they are the stationery buyer, aren't they?)

Agreement - *'Consensus ad idem'*

This is one of the many Latin phrases of which the law is fond. It can be translated as 'an agreement on the same thing' (sometimes you will see it translated as 'a meeting of the minds'). Essentially it means that both parties to the contract are in agreement as to the nature of the subject (i.e. the product or service being bought and sold) of the contract. This is easy when you are discussing the contract face-to-face with a seller with the subject of the contract at hand. It is less easy when you are buying by description over the telephone or from a catalogue, when offeror and offeree might have entirely different conceptions of the nature (e.g. size, robustness, material, etc.) of the item.

Obviously it is very difficult to prove what was in your mind at any one time, and it is for this reason that it is usual to reserve the right to take a suitable time to inspect items bought by description to make sure that they are as you intended. Also, most catalogues have phrases such as 'money refunded if not absolutely delighted'.

This saves a great deal of time and trouble with legal action in the event of a distant customer deciding that the item, upon receipt, does not bear much resemblance to the photograph or drawing in the catalogue.

Consideration

This is what the buyer gives to the seller in exchange for the goods or services. It is usually money although the law only states that consideration must be 'something of value' thus recognising barter, swapping and exchanging one service for another or a exchanging a service for goods, or vice-versa. In the great majority of instances in commercial purchasing, however, consideration is the payment.

Legality

The subject of the contract must be legal. It is not possible to make a binding contract for an illegal purpose (e.g. for the purchase of Class A drugs), not that this should be relevant to commercial purchasing. The law does not recognise gaming contracts (e.g. the Lottery, betting, football pools, etc.). It is perfectly legal to enter into them, but you cannot take legal action in the event of e.g. non-payment of winnings. Again this should not be relevant to commercial purchasing.

It is worth making some general points which are relevant to the formation of contracts.

      ☐   A contract need not be in any particular form. There is no special document required to make a contract legally binding.

The contract does not even have to be in writing at all – the law recognises oral contracts. Unfortunately, however, if a dispute arises over an oral contract, it is virtually impossible to bring a successful action in court. The court would say that the dispute was 'one person's word against another's' and would not be able to decide either way. The only way to win a claim relating to an oral contract is to have 'substantive witness', i.e. someone who is not involved with either party who has witnessed the entire transaction (it would usually be quite impossible to find such a person. Other employees of your company, or the seller's, are not independent and someone hearing your end of a telephone conversation has not heard the entire transaction.) The moral here is ensure all contracts are in writing and, if you have a verbal agreement, commit it to writing as soon as possible.

Privity of contract

There is a principle inherent in law that only a party to the contract may sue or be sued upon it, a principle established by the case of *Tweddle vs Atkinson (1861)*.

Here, the father and future father-in-law of a bridegroom-to-be (the plaintiff) a sum of money prior to the marriage. The future father-in-law died without making the payment and the plaintiff sued his estate for the money. The court held that, despite the fact that the plaintiff was the intended beneficiary of the contract, he was not party to it and could not, therefore, enforce it.

There are exceptions to this principle, however.

Firstly, there is the matter of 'collateral contracts'. This is when a supplier, such as a car dealer, provides for the end user a product bearing the manufacturer's guarantee or warranty. This principle was established by the case of *Shanklin Pier vs Detel Products ltd. (1951)*.

Here, a purchaser placed a contract for the painting of a pier with a contractor, and stipulated that a certain brand of paint be used because the paint supplier has said that it would last seven years. In the event, it only lasted three months and it was held that the purchaser had a direct claim against the paint manufacturer collaterally to any claim that the contractor might have.

Secondly, there is the Contracts (Rights of Third Parties) Act that came into effect on 11 May 2000. This lays down the principle that a third party may enforce rights under a contract where:

☐   that party is expressly given the right to do so under the contract.

- the contract purports to confer a benefit on that party.

- the parties to the contract have not made it clear that they intended to exclude that third party from having the right to enforce.

There is more detail in the Act, as you would expect, that is beyond our scope here, but much of it relates to such issues as identification of the third parties, the concept of positive and negative benefit, the court having limited authority to reduce third party rights and the fact that third party rights cannot be rescinded or varied without their consent.

However, the Act does not apply to:

- Bills of exchange, promissory notes and other negotiable instruments.

- Company memoranda or articles of association.

- Contracts of employment.

- Some contracts for the carriage of goods.

The Buyer's Role in Preparing Contracts

As we have already said, many buyers take the view that they do not need to know much, if anything, about the law of contract because, if they get into difficulties they can always contact a lawyer who will be able to solve the problem. However, the buyer is, or should be, the first point of contact between his/her company and the seller and the law exists to reinforce and support the agreement reached between buyer and seller.

For this reason, buyers need to know what the law requires of them because, having reached agreement with the seller, often verbally, the buyer is charged with committing the agreement to writing. It is of the utmost importance that the written agreement conforms to the requirement of the law in all respects.

Additionally, there may be times when the buyer has to collaborate with his/her company lawyer or legal department to devise the terms and conditions that will appear on documentation.

The buyer's role in this respect will be to input information on the purchasing requirements of the terms and conditions, but some knowledge and understanding of legal requirements will make the process much easier and faster.

Terms and Conditions of Contract

These make up the 'small print' on the reverse of many companies' purchase orders and other documents and, in practice, are ignored by many buyers. Potentially, however, they are important and we will examine the nature of this importance. Remember, buyers have terms and conditions of purchase; sellers have terms and conditions of sale.

What are terms and conditions?

In law, the word used should be 'term'. In practice, the words 'term' and 'condition' have different meanings. As we will see shortly a term can be either a 'condition' or a 'warranty'.

So what exactly is a term?

Essentially, terms form the details of a contract, and can be seen as a statement by either party of the 'rules' by which they intend the 'game' of contracting to be played. The fact that they are often relegated to the reverse of the order or quotation (if they appear at all) and are frequently printed in typeface so small as to be barely legible, causes many people to regard them as being irrelevant. This view, however, is mistakenly so. The fact is that the terms and conditions are part of an offer or counter-offer and can have the effect of rendering what was intended to be 'acceptance' a 'counter-offer'.

This is because the buyer's terms and conditions will be worded in a way which protects the buyer's interests, and the seller's terms and conditions will usually protect the seller's interests and, in practice, there will almost always be a conflict between the two sets of terms and conditions.

Terms, conditions and warranties

Earlier we made the point that, legally speaking, we should use the word 'term' rather than 'condition' as both have a slightly different meaning. A term can be either:

☐ a condition – these are terms which are crucial to the performance of the contract

or

☐ a warranty (not to be confused with a type of guarantee). These are terms of lesser importance to the performance of the contract.

This distinction is important because of the difference in remedies (solutions or settlements) in the event of a breach. If a supplier breaches a condition, the buyer may take one or a combination of the following courses of action:

- Rescind the contract (return both parties to where they were before the contract was made).

- Repudiate the contract and avoid the outstanding obligations (duties of the contract).

- Seek an order from the court for 'specific performance' (force the supplier to perform their contractual obligations).

- Receive damages (set by the court as compensation for the breach).

If a supplier breaches a warranty the buyer can only sue for damages and the court would only award these so as to compensate for losses directly associated with the breach.

Whether or not a term is a condition or a warranty would be decided by the court in the event of litigation.

'Express' or 'implied' terms

- Express terms are clearly stated and agreed between the parties.

- Implied terms are not always mentioned but are assumed to exist and can form part of the contract. This might appear to be a difficult notion but an example would be the right of the seller to sell the goods. This would be assumed (by both parties) to exist without being discussed.

Express terms

Some matters are so fundamental that, if the parties have not agreed to them, no contract can exist. It is entirely up to the parties to decide what further matters to cover in their agreement, and major commercial contracts generally go very much further and tend to go into great detail.

Typically, express terms might deal with the subject matter of the contract, the price, any price variation clause, a *force majeure* clause, etc. Probably, the best way of illustrating this is by listing terms and conditions with which we, as buyers, are familiar. If we had a major capital contract, which requires a supplier to design, manufacture and supply a piece of equipment, then the following table shows a typical list of matters which are expressly provided for in the agreement:

	Term	Outline of Provisions
1	The contract	Statement of purpose of contract and brief summary of parties' respective responsibilities
2	The parties	Warranties as to: • Parties' contractual capacity and internal approvals • Seller's skill, expertise and availability of personnel • Buyer's access funds
3.	Performance of contract	Standard of performance required of seller Compliance with applicable laws and regulations Subcontracting of work by seller Timetable for completion of various stages of the work Appointment of each party's project manager and the procedure for changing them
4.	The goods	Specification - statement of buyer's requirements Design - seller's obligations; approval by buyers; extent of buyer's involvement Materials - sources, origins and standards of components and materials Manufacture - place of manufacture; buyer's right to inspect Testing - testing programme; performance criteria; buyer's right to be present New technology - seller to incorporate any new technology which becomes available after the contract was made Acceptance - written acceptance of goods by buyer Warranties - seller's obligations if goods fail to meet performance criteria or are defective
5.	Delivery	Time and place of deliveries. If the time of performance is considered to be important, the parties must agree that 'time shall be of the essence' because the general contractual principle is that it is not of the essence. Responsibility for delivery costs Consequences of late delivery, including liquidated damages
6.	Title and risk	Time of transfer of title to the goods Retention of title provisions Time of transfer of risk in the goods

7.	Price	Determination of price: price escalation, cost overruns, acceleration payments Payment for work outside original scope of the contract Buyer's right of audit
8.	Payments	Method of payment Stage payments Retention of part of price by buyer Interest on late payments
9.	Guarantees of performance	Buyer and/or seller to provide a guarantee of performance from parent company or bank, or else a performance bond
10.	Termination	Circumstances in which contract terminates, e.g. • Cancellation by buyer • In event of seller's default • In event of buyer's failure to pay • In event of insolvency of party Consequences of termination: ownership of goods, payment for work completed Identification of terms which survive termination
11.	Patents	Identification of relevant patents Right to use patents owned by parties Responsibility for obtaining patent licenses from third party Responsibility for ensuring no patent infringements Ownership of patents developed for the purpose of the contract
12,	Liabilities	Apportionment of liabilities under the contract Exclusion of certain liabilities Indemnities against certain types of claims or losses Force majeure provisions
13.	Insurance	Requirements for parties to ensure against certain risks levels of insurance Responsibility for insuring the goods
14.	Confidentiality	Parties to maintain the confidentiality of the contract and all information acquired in the course of it Exceptions for public information, disclosures to government departments or as required by law
15.	Assignment	Whether either party is permitted to assign the contract: the procedure for doing so.
16.	Arbitration	Disputes to be settled by arbitration

| 17. | Law and jurisdiction | Choice of governing law; submission by parties to the jurisdiction of the courts |
| 18. | Notices | Names and addresses for service of formal notices under contract Change of those names and addresses |

Figure 1: Sample list of a contract for the design, manufacture and supply of a piece of capital equipment

Contentious terms and 'boilerplate'

The provisions relating to the goods, price and payment are, of course, the commercial heart of the contract. They will have been the focus of the parties' technical and commercial representatives, and if these crucial matters cannot be agreed, no contract will be concluded. These will usually be 'conditions'.

Terms 14-18 are often referred to as 'legal boilerplate'. These terms are not usually contentious and it is unlikely that the negotiation will fail because the parties cannot agree on these provisions.

Apart from price, the most contentious issues will probably have been the seller's warranties in relation to the goods, the consequences of late delivery, the provisions of guarantees of performance, termination, liabilities and insurance. It is interesting to note that all of these terms are concerned with what happens if something goes wrong: if nothing goes wrong, it will not be necessary to refer to them.

Implied terms

Sometimes a term which has not been expressly agreed between the parties will, nevertheless, be implied into a contract. There are two situations in which this can happen. The first is where the parties must have intended that term to be included even though they did not say so. Another way of putting this is that, to be implied, a term must be so obvious that it goes without saying. This is known as the officious bystander test and means that, if a third party were standing by, listening to the two parties cementing the contract, and suggested a term, the parties would respond with a common 'of course'. Conditions may be implied from general custom and practice in the particular business or from previous usage between the parties.

The second is where an Act of Parliament requires a term to be implied into a contract of that type. An example of this would be Sale of Goods legislation (see later) where the following are imputed (in other words, implied) into contracts unless there are clauses to the contrary:

    ☐   that the seller has good title to the goods.

◻   that the goods match the description and any samples supplied.

◻   that they are of satisfactory quality.

◻   that they are fit for all purposes for which the goods are commonly supplied.

The 'Battle of the Forms'

This is a phenomenon of which we should be aware, as well as being aware of its consequences.

The name arises from the documents (or 'forms') which, in some situations, can go back and forth between buyer and seller. It concerns the fact that, if the various forms (quotation, order, acknowledgement, etc.) differ from each other in some way, usually because of conflicts in the terms and conditions, they will constitute counter offers rather than acceptance, meaning that formal acceptance of the original offer never takes place and no contract exists. For example:

◻   A quotation is received from a supplier, which is an offer.

◻   A purchase order is sent to the supplier, but, while the main part is in agreement with the quotation, the terms differ and so the order constitutes a counter offer.

◻   The supplier then acknowledges the order on a document containing its own terms, and this is another counter offer, remembering that any counter offer has to be accepted for a legally-binding contract to exist.

The rule is as follows: If no query has arisen during the performance of the contract, and the seller delivers the goods to the buyer, if the buyer accepts them, a legally-binding contract is deemed to have come into existence with the terms prevailing being contained on the last document that passed between the parties. This is sometimes known as 'the last document rule', and buyers should be very careful of it because, often, the last document is likely to be either the seller's acknowledgement or advice note, both of which will probably contain the seller's terms. The battle of the forms is illustrated in the following diagram, which shows a typical flow of documents or 'forms' that might pass between buyer and seller.

The example shown will hopefully clarify the situation (remember that terms and conditions are an integral part of any offer, etc.). It shows the various documents which pass between a buyer and seller and shows the legal significance. Many people believe that the situation illustrated here is a fairly common occurrence.

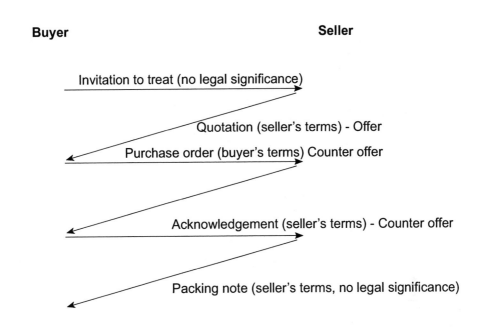

Buyer **Seller**

Invitation to treat (no legal significance)

Quotation (seller's terms) - Offer

Purchase order (buyer's terms) Counter offer

Acknowledgement (seller's terms) - Counter offer

Packing note (seller's terms, no legal significance)

Figure 2: Battle of the Forms'

We should note that no 'acceptance' has taken place. However, if there is no query or problem, the goods will be delivered and, if acceptable, will be accepted. The question then arises as to what, in this situation, the legal position is. There is a legally binding contract, because the conduct of both parties (delivery and acceptance) would lead one to presume that there was one.

The terms binding on the contract are contained on the last document to pass between the parties (in the illustration these are the seller's terms).

We should note that this rule only applies where there has been no previous formal 'acceptance', so that in the example shown in this next illustration, the 'last document' rule does not apply.

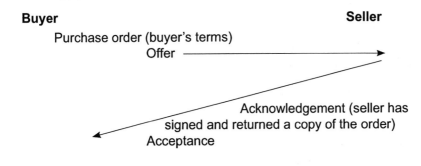

Buyer **Seller**

Purchase order (buyer's terms)
Offer

Acknowledgement (seller has
signed and returned a copy of the order)
Acceptance

Figure 3: Alternative 'Battle of the Forms'

The following should be noted:

Once 'acceptance' has been deemed to take place, no subsequent document has any legal significance. Many people appear to believe that counter offers can take place after acceptance, but this is not so. Providing all of the other requirements for a contract to exist (consideration, capacity, intention, etc.) are in place, once acceptance has occurred, a legally binding contract exists. This is the point at which the contract is said to come into being, and is of great importance.

As stated above, the 'last document' rule only applies if there has been no prior acceptance. Again, many people appear to believe that the 'last document' rule applies in all situations. This is not so.

Buyers who are aware of the above situations will try to ensure that the battle of the forms does not arise, and that contracts are awarded subject to their terms by:

    ◻   Sending enquiries with the buyer's terms and conditions and stipulating that potential sellers must respond by completing and returning a copy of the enquiry document.

    ◻   Sending acknowledgement copies of each purchase order which the supplier is supposed to sign and return.

    ◻   Negotiating and agreeing with the supplier the nature of the contract, including terms and conditions. This would be the preferred option when entering into large contracts that involve large sums of money and/or long term contracts.

We should note that dispensing with our terms and conditions might avoid the 'battle of the forms', but will almost certainly result in the contract being bound by the seller's terms and conditions and would, almost certainly, disadvantage the buyer.

Many suppliers are only too aware of what the buyer is seeking to do and will (e.g.) return the buyer's enquiry with their own document attached. This latter document would have precedence over previous documents.

However, we should always try to ensure that our company's standard/special conditions of purchase are accepted.

The main legal case relating to the 'battle of the forms' is that of *Butler Machine Tool vs Ex-Cell-O Corporation (England) Ltd. (1979)*.

In this case, Butler Machine Tool Company, the supplier, quoted for a machine tool on 23 May 1969, at a price of £75 535, and delivery to be within 10 months from the date of order. The contractual terms included within the quotation were stated expressly to prevail (supersede) over any contractual terms contained in the buyer's order.

One of Butler's standard terms was a contract price adjustment or price variation clause which allowed them to vary the contract price if their costs changed.

Ex-Cell-O, the purchaser, ordered the machine on 27 May 1969, but their order included their own terms of contract. These terms did not include a price variation clause and the delivery date was changed to 10-11 months. Their order form also included an acknowledgement slip. This slip was returned to Ex-Cell-O on 5 June 1969, and it stated "Acknowledgement: please sign and return to Ex-Cell-O. We accept your order on the terms and conditions stated therein - and undertake to deliver by ....date....signed."

The machine was ready for delivery by September 1970, but Ex-Cell-O delayed taking delivery because of necessary arrangements to their production schedule. They eventually took delivery in November 1970, and Butler claimed £2 892 due under their contract price variation clause. Ex-Cell-O refused to pay the sum arguing that the contract was based on their terms.

The court held that there was indeed no price variation clause present in the contract and so Ex-Cell-O did not have to pay the additional £2 892. This was because the supplier's terms did not apply to the contract. Butler's quote was an offer, Ex-Cell-O's order was a counter offer which was accepted by the return of the acknowledgement slip.

Under English law, if the acknowledgement slip had not been returned by the supplier, acceptance could still have been made by the conduct of the supplier, i.e. by their actions.

We should note that, in this example, no formal acceptance has taken place. However, if the goods have been delivered and accepted, a legally-binding contract is deemed to exist with the binding terms contained in the last document. In this example, the prevailing terms will be the seller's.

It will almost certainly be against the interests of the company to allow contracts to be awarded subject to a seller's terms and conditions because these will have been developed to protect the seller's interests, which, despite modern thinking on collaboration and partnerships, would almost certainly be at odds with your interests. We should therefore try to ensure that contracts are subject to our terms and conditions. If we do not have any (as some companies do not), we are leaving our company wide open to being taken advantage of by suppliers.

It can be argued that, in many cases, terms and conditions are not important. For example, when a private individual buys merchandise from a shop terms and conditions are hardly ever mentioned, although they are becoming increasingly important in major domestic purchases. However, in commercial practice it may well be the case that terms and conditions are ignored when we are buying low-value items from tried and tested suppliers, but when we are looking to award multi-million pound contracts, terms and conditions become very important indeed. In these situations, if there are disputes, the buyer and the supplier should negotiate until they have a set of terms and conditions that both parties can work with.

We should always try to ensure that the company's standard/special conditions of purchase are accepted. These may include:

Definitions

☐ The full name of your company as well as that of the seller.

☐ A full description of the item.

Acknowledgement

☐ A stipulation that your purchase order should be acknowledged in writing.

Variations

☐ A stipulation that no variations to the contract are acceptable without your written agreement.

Inspection/testing

☐ A term that sets out to allow your company adequate time to carry out thorough inspection of incoming goods, where considered necessary. Typically, this would be a minimum of three days.

Delivery/packing

☐ A stipulation that this should be in accordance with the instructions contained in the purchase order.

Passing of property

☐ An indication of when the company believes that the item should become the buyer's property. Typically, this would be when the goods have been physically accepted and have been certified as being satisfactory. Care is required here, because many suppliers will insist that property only passes when the goods have been paid for in full. This is likely to be a rather different time from 'satisfactory delivery'. Also, some suppliers try to impose what is generally referred to as a 'Romalpa clause' (after the name of one of the parties in the original case). This would stipulate that property only passes to the buyer upon payment in full, no matter what has happened to the goods prior to that time. This means that, where such a term were applied, it would be possible that goods could be delivered to the buyer, assembled into the buyer's finished product and sold to a customer, and if payment had not been made to the original supplier, the goods would remain that supplier's property until payment had been made.

In this situation, the principle would still apply even though it would be virtually impossible to identify the exact original goods! Fortunately, perhaps, such clauses are invoked infrequently today.

Time

☐ It is usual to include a clause stating that 'Time shall be of the essence of the order'. Without such a clause it is virtually impossible to take legal action against a supplier for late delivery.

Damage/loss in transit

☐ It is usual to include a clause that states that the seller should be liable for any such damage or loss.

Payment

☐ The buyer should include a clause stating the terms of payment preferred by the buyer's organisation, for example 'that payment will be made thirty days after the end of the month following submission of an invoice by the seller'. An example of this would be that, if a supplier's invoice were presented on, say, 8 September, the buyer's company would undertake to settle it at the end of October.

☐ A clause stating the preferred method of payment may also be included. Examples include credit transfer or cheque. Such a clause takes on a greater degree of importance with overseas purchases.

Assignment/subcontracting

☐ It is usual to state that no part of the contract shall be given to a third party without the buyer's written consent. If some element of sub-contracting is intended by the seller or main contractor, the buyer needs to be made aware of it, so that some form of supplier appraisal of the sub-contractor may be carried out. This also ensures that an unapproved sub-contractor is not used by the main contractor.

Arbitration

- Buyers often insert a clause stipulating that any disputes would be settled by arbitration rather than litigation.

Rejection

- It is usual to insert a clause to establish rules for the possible rejection of goods supplied, i.e. the conditions under which the buyer believes that rejection of goods supplied should take place, as well as the time that should be allowed to do this. This is usually linked to the amount of time that the buyer believes is necessary for adequate inspection of goods, and takes on greater importance when the subject of the contract is work performed rather than the supply of goods.

'Model' (or 'Standard') Forms of Contract

The previous section may have given the impression that terms and conditions are negotiated afresh between buyer and seller for every contract. This is usually not the case. Instead, buyers will usually seek to use a set of standard terms that exists already, although in some cases these may be modified to suit particular circumstances. The standard terms generally originate as follows:

- From the buying or selling company – most companies will have developed a set of standard terms that, it is deemed, will suit their needs in most situations. As has been stated previously, a buyer should always try to ensure that his/her terms prevail because the seller's terms will almost definitely not protect the buyer's interests.

- From CIPS – CIPS have developed a standard set of terms that are widely held to be excellent. They are available to members via the CIPS web-site (www.cips.org) although a fee is payable. In the absence of your own terms these would usually prove highly acceptable.

- From trade associations or other bodies; these are often useful for specific types of contract. Examples (not an exhaustive list) of such sets of standard terms are:

  - BEAMA (British Electrical and Allied Manufacturers' Association), an organisation that has a number of formulae that attempt (usually successfully) to measure inflation during the running time of contracts. A specific BEAMA formula may be applied to a specific type of contract.

- RIBA (Royal Institution of British Architects) has also developed a standard set of terms, in this case, to cover construction contracts.

The Rights and Obligations of Buyer and Seller in Contracts

Buying and selling is seen by lawyers as a process of creating and completing contracts. This is not the way in which buyers and sellers normally see it, but lawyers are usually called in when things go wrong. It should be pointed out that the great majority of disputes between buyer and seller are resolved by negotiation between the parties, but if this does not succeed and the matter reaches a court of law, what the courts have to establish before reaching a decision is what rights and obligations were agreed to in the contract.

Contracts are simply legally enforceable agreements. Millions are made every day. If you call in at a shop and buy the morning newspaper, in law you are making a contract. The question that would arise in this situation is 'What legal enforceability would there be?'

It may be hard to see how that applies. You don't pay for the paper until you have it, and perhaps you would not get far from the shop without paying for it. But, in principle, this transaction is a contract, as are all the other purchases we make in shops or on buses or railways or airlines.

Most contracts are made between two persons, the buyer and the seller. Some contracts involve more than two persons.

Persons in contract law are either human beings with contractual capacity or organisations with contractual capacity, such as registered companies (see under 'capacity' above). Contractual capacity is the ability to make a contract which is binding in law. The law protects people who are drunk or very young or have mental disorders, by restricting their contractual capacity.

Rights and obligations resulting from a contract exist only between the two (or more) persons who are parties to the contract. A party to a contract is a person (as defined above) who has accepted rights and obligations in accordance with a contract to which that person has freely agreed. A contract does not normally confer any rights or impose any obligations on other persons – 'third party', that is to say, people or organisations which are not one of the (usually) two persons who have agreed to the contract.

Each party to a contact has the obligation to do whatever the contract says. For instance, if B orders 1,000 widgets, in accordance with an attached specification, from S at the price of £20 per thousand, for delivery during the first week of April, to be paid for within four weeks of invoice date, and if S accepts this order so that a contract comes into existence, then S's obligations are: to deliver 1,000 widgets which conform to specification, during the first week of April and to send an invoice for them to B.

B's rights are for S to do the above.

B's obligations are: to accept the goods if delivered on time and to specification, and to pay for them within four weeks of invoice date if the invoice price is, as per the purchase order, £20 per 1,000.

S's rights are for B to do the above.

Other rights and obligations may exist even in this simple example, but only if they are spelled out in the contract or assumed by the law to be implied by it. We will return to that shortly. Let us first consider what the legal position is if either party fails to meet contractual obligations.

In the example above, B might find that 1,000 widgets are not required after all, so a letter is sent cancelling the order. But B has no legal right to do this, since the contract binds them to accept the goods. S would be within their rights in refusing to agree to cancellation, delivering the goods and insisting on payment. If B failed to pay they could be taken to court where legal expenses and time wasted might add considerably to the cost of the transaction.

Orders do sometimes have to be amended or cancelled, but this has to be done with the consent of the other party who is entitled to payment for work already done or materials already purchased in accordance with the contract.

What if S fails to deliver at the due date, or delivers the wrong quantity, or the goods delivered do not conform to the specification, or the price charged is not the agreed price of £20 per 1,000?

The last point is straightforward. Since both parties have agreed to a price, that is the price payable. S has no legal right to increase the price, even if costs increase or if a mistake is found in the original estimate, except with the consent of B, the other party.

The other points all involve failure on the part of S to do what has been agreed in the contract and it has to be asked how serious this failure is. Lawyers distinguish between a condition, defined in the Sale of Goods Act as a term of the contract that goes to the heart or 'root' of a contract, 'breach of which may give rise to a right to treat the contract as repudiated', and a warranty, defined as a breach of a term, which does not entitle the injured party to treat the contract as repudiated but may give rise to a claim for damages (see earlier in this chapter).

Treating the contract as 'repudiated' means ending the contract so that neither party has any contractual obligations, although either party may be entitled to compensation. It should be noted that, as well as repudiation, breach of a condition allows the injured party then option of continuing with the contract and suing for damages instead. If breach of warranty occurs, the contract is still in existence, but the injured party may be entitled to compensation in the form of damages.

Relevant Legislation

For many years, indeed centuries, the principle of *caveat emptor* guided all contracts. This is a principle that dates back to antiquity and translates as 'let the buyer beware', thus firmly placing the onus on the buyer to take all reasonable care in entering into contracts, so that their interests are protected. In more recent times it became apparent that, in the sale of goods, products were becoming more complex and difficult, if not impossible, to examine in any meaningful way.

This view led legislators to realise that more protection was required for buyers entering into a contract, the presumption being that the seller knows the product because they are selling it but the buyer was at a disadvantage because they had no real knowledge of it and that inspection would not identify such issues as reliability and whether the product would perform its required purpose adequately. In the light of this view, it was decided that some form of protection was needed for buyers and this first took place with the Sale of Goods Act of 1893.

The 1893 Act has since been superseded and today, the principal laws or Acts of Parliament which relate to purchasing and supply are:

- The Sale of Goods Act, 1979,

- The Supply of Goods and Services Act, 1982,

- The Sale and Supply of Goods Act, 1994,

- The Unfair Contract Terms Act, 1977.

The intention here is merely to give a 'flavour' of how each of these Acts protects the buyer. It should be noted that, whilst these Acts afford some protection to the seller, their chief role is to protect the buyer.

These Acts have been passed by Parliament as a result of a growing recognition, in recent years, that the buyer in any transaction is the weaker party, and therefore requires a level of protection which basic contract law cannot give. Such 'weakness' arises because:

☐ The buyer often cannot see the goods to be bought and, therefore, cannot examine them.

  and

☐ If the buyer could see the goods, they may not possess the knowledge to be able to evaluate their quality or their ability to perform the function required. This is especially true when complex pieces of machinery are being purchased.

☐ Another Act of Parliament which can protect the buyer is the Consumer Protection Act. The detail of this Act is beyond our scope here, but one of its provisions, for instance, makes it a criminal offence to supply goods without adequate safety warnings.

The Sale of Goods Act, 1979

This is the most important law relating to purchasing and supply and replaced the 1893 Act of the same name. The main provisions of this Act are as follows:

☐ The Act only covers the sale of goods. In other words, barter transactions or the provision of services in exchange for money are not covered although these types of transaction are perfectly capable of being legally binding contracts under contract law.

☐ It lays down rules governing the transfer of ownership of goods and recognises that:

   • the buyer is buying the right of ownership of goods.

   • if someone does not have ownership of the goods (even though the goods may be in the person's possession) they cannot sell them; this is known as the rule of 'nemo dat quod non habet' which loosely translated means that you cannot sell what is not yours to sell (a more literal translation would be 'no one can give what they do not have'). This rule is usually known as the 'nemo dat' rule.

☐ It stipulates that goods must be of 'merchantable quality'. This essentially means that the goods are of the type of quality and appearance that you would expect to have when buying goods commercially.

◻   It stipulates that goods must be 'fit for the purpose' when:

- The purpose is expressed or implied by the buyer. 'Express' means where the buyer has told the seller what the goods are required for and what function they are required to perform. 'Implied' means that any reasonable person would know what the goods are required for; for example, when buying a car, the buyer does not need to tell the seller that it is required for travelling in – any reasonable person would know that without being told.

- The seller is selling the goods in the normal course of their business.

This last point is very important, because it means that if you ask a seller to recommend something for a particular purpose and it fails to work, provided the seller was selling the item as a normal part of his business (in other words, this rule does not apply to a private individual or a business selling the item as a 'sideline'), the seller would be liable in law for the lack of performance or poor performance.

The Act stipulates that goods will correspond with any sample used to obtain the sale. In other words, if a seller sends you a sample and, based on its quality/fitness for the purpose etc. you place an order for a large quantity and the quality of the main batch does not match that of the sample, the seller is liable in law and would be required to correct the matter.

The Supply of Goods and Services Act, 1982

The main essence of this Act is to make the main aspects of the Sale of Goods Act also cover the sale of services, these contracts being excluded from the 1979 Act. This is very important for buyers in today's commercial world where the purchase of services is becoming increasingly common.

The Sale and Supply of Goods Act, 1994

This has had the effect of modifying the 1979 Act in some important respects. The chief of these relates to 'merchantable quality'. The new Act states that when the seller sells goods in the course of a business, there is an implied term that the goods supplied under the contract are of satisfactory quality, not 'merchantable quality', as found in the 1979 Act.

The definition of satisfactory quality is important and is wider than merchantable quality in the following respects.

The Act states that goods are of satisfactory quality if they meet the standard that a reasonable person would regard as satisfactory, taking account of any description of the goods, the price (if relevant) and all other relevant circumstances.

For the purposes of this Act, the quality of goods includes their state and condition and the following (among others) are, in appropriate cases, aspects of the quality of goods:

- Fitness for all the purposes for which goods of the kind in question are commonly supplied. This does not mean that they will be suitable for a specific purpose under specific non-general conditions.

- Appearance and finish.

- Freedom from minor defects.

- Safety and durability.

The term 'satisfactory quality' does not extend to any matter making the quality of goods unsatisfactory which is specifically drawn to the buyer's attention before the contract is made, where the buyer examines the goods before the contract is made, when that examination ought to reveal the fault/defect/problem or in the case of a contract for sale by sample, where the fault/defect/problem would have been apparent on a reasonable examination of the sample. In respect of sale by sample, the Act has the following provisions:

- The bulk must correspond with the sample in terms of quality.

- The buyer must have reasonable opportunity of comparing the bulk with the sample.

- The goods must be free from any defect making their quality unsatisfactory, which a reasonable examination of the sample would not reveal.

Other implied terms are:

- The seller has the right to sell the goods.

- No third party has any rights over the goods which the seller has not disclosed to the buyer.

- The buyer will enjoy 'quiet possession' of the goods.

The Unfair Contract Terms Act, 1977

This introduces the concept of reasonableness into contract terms. In practice this often concerns exclusion clauses. In general terms, however, if a seller puts any clause into a contract which is considered 'unreasonable' or 'unfair' or is the result of duress, the court would insist that it be removed. Note, however, that the Act can work the other way round also and, if a buyer stipulated that, for example, 'payment shall take place 150 days after presentation of the invoice by the seller' the court might insist upon its removal.

The definition of duress used to be limited to threats of physical violence but now also includes 'illegitimate threats to goods', that is to say, economic duress, this latter being of particular interest to supply chain specialists. If duress is to be actionable, two criteria must be satisfied:

☐ Did the victim of the duress complain at the time?

☐ Did the victim intend to repudiate the agreement?

The concept of 'economic duress' was illustrated by the case of *Atlas Express ltd. vs Kafco (Importers and Distributors Ltd.).(1989):*

In this case, the plaintiff company, Atlas Express Ltd, contracted with the defendants, Kafco, to transport cartons of basketware for them to retail premises nationwide. The agreed rate was £1.10 per carton, the plaintiffs' expectation being that each load would comprise 400-600 cartons. The first load contained only 200 cartons and the plaintiffs refused to carry any more loads unless the defendants agreed to a minimum price of £440 per load. Unable to find an alternative carrier - and thus dependent on the plaintiffs, the defendants agreed reluctantly to pay the new rate.

When they subsequently refused to pay, the plaintiffs sued to enforce the new agreement. The Commercial Court, dismissing the claim, held that the pressure applied by the plaintiffs to force the defendants to renegotiate the contract was economic duress, which vitiated (see 'Vitiating factors' later in the chapter) the contract.

Dispute Resolution

It is easy and tempting to suppose that every time you disagree with a supplier you take them to court. The fact is, however, that this action ('litigation') is usually the last resort. The options open to the buyer to resolve disputes are as follows, in ascending order of cost, difficulty and time consumption:

Negotiation

The vast majority of claims and disputes can be settled by amicable negotiation leading to an agreement. This is the quickest and least costly method of settling disputes, and as every buyer should know, is the preferred first course of action should a dispute with a supplier arise.

Adjudication

This is a process of expert determination. The expert is appointed by agreement between the parties, either generally or to decide a particular issue. Provided the expert keeps within the terms of the appointment and shows no bias, there is no restriction on the way a decision can be reached.

Adjudication is less formal, and generally quicker and less costly than arbitration and litigation. If the contract provides for the expert determination to be final and binding, in other words, if both parties agree, a court will not interfere with the decision reached.

Arbitration

Arbitration is more formal than adjudication, and resembles litigation, although will generally be less costly. It is a semi-judicial process, with evidence being heard. The hearing of evidence is an important distinction between arbitration and adjudication. Arbitration may also involve aspects of law, because, today, many arbitrators are experienced lawyers, whereas adjudication is more concerned with the facts of the dispute and could be likened to negotiation with a referee, although this is not a official description. Unlike the adjudicator, an arbitrator cannot be sued for negligence. If the parties to a contract are unable to settle a dispute by arbitration, then there is no alternative but to enter into litigation.

Litigation

Litigation is the term used to describe dispute resolution in the courts. It tends to be a time-consuming, costly and complex process, and is often used only as a last resort. Under English law, cases between businesses are usually heard in the high court, often by a single judge, although the normal appeal process for a party not satisfied with the decision via the Court of Appeal, and finally the House of Lords, applies.

You should note that both adjudication and arbitration are often known collectively as 'Alternative Dispute Resolution' or ADR, and many companies see it as a preferred route to try to solve disputed before litigation becomes inevitable. This is because enforcing cases in the normal civil courts can be a lengthy and time consuming business. There are alternative forms of dispute resolution available to commercial and other organisations in the United Kingdom. Principally these involve some form of binding arbitration or conciliation process.

For arbitration an independent arbitrator is usually chosen after the dispute arises, although not always. For example, an insurance policy usually contains a clause providing for this method of settling any disputes which may arise.

The arbitrator is appointed to hear arguments presented by the parties. The type of arbitrator chosen will depend on the nature of the case. The arbitrator's main role is to try to effect a settlement between the parties rather than to impose a judgement as to who is right or wrong.

Arbitration may arise in different ways.

- **by contract** - the parties may by contract include a clause agreeing to refer any dispute to an arbitrator; this person may also be named in the contract. Almost all vehicle insurance policies have such a clause.

- **by ruling of the court** - the judge may decide to refer the dispute to arbitration.

- **by statute** - for example, under the Marine Insurance Act 1905, maritime disputes are to be settled by arbitration. London is an international arbitration centre, with 70-80% of all disputes being referred to it.

The advantages of arbitration, and why it is preferred to court action are:

- it is less formal than litigation - the informal atmosphere and straightforward procedure is often preferred by parties involved.

- it is flexible - it avoids the rigidity which the doctrine of judicial precedent imposes on the traditional courts.

- there is greater specialist knowledge - for example, more commercially-aware expert staff are involved.

- it avoids publicity - proceedings are held in private.

- it is often less expensive - the procedure is cheaper, although the costs of the arbitrator may be quite high, and the time spent on an arbitration is often less than on a civil litigation case in the Commercial Court. Discouraging legal representation potentially reduces the fees further.

- it is quick.

- parties can select and stipulate the identity of the arbitrator. If the parties cannot agree on who is to be appointed, then the Arbitration Act gives the courts the power to do so.

- it is regulated by statute, the Arbitration Act 1996.

- an arbitrator's award may be enforced in the same way as a High Court judgement. This means that the courts allow the parties to settle their own disputes, but at the same time maintain a supervisory role.

Arbitration does have disadvantages, however, which are:

- arbitrators are often not skilled in applying or interpreting the law although, increasingly, commercial arbitrators are also senior lawyers.

- there are no formal rules - discretion can lead to inconsistent and unpredictable decisions.

- the parties may still end up in a court of law, although at least they must go to arbitration first, especially if there is a *Scott vs Avery* clause.

- appeal is only possible on a point of law, not a point of fact.

It is worth noting that arbitration is often used to resolve disputes of an international nature.

Another form of arbitration is the **small claims court**.

Since 1973 there has been an arbitration service within the County Court via the small claims procedure. Registrars, who tend to be solicitors, hear cases; they listen mainly to debt cases up to £5 000.

In addition to the small claims court, or as an alternative to it, many consumer organisations operate forms of arbitration, but most are run by the various industry bodies such as ABTA (Association of British Travel Agents), which looks after arbitration in the travel industry.

Various bodies will also act as conciliators in order to facilitate the parties reaching an agreement. This is different from arbitration, where the arbitrator makes a decision for one party or the other. In conciliation the parties are brought together in an attempt to reach their own decision with the aid of the conciliation body. An example of this in the case of employment is ACAS (Arbitration, Conciliation and Advice Service).

It is worth noting that you might see the term 'mediation' used as an alternative to ADR.

Vitiating Factors

By vitiating factors, we are considering the various factors which can make a contract, or a particular provision in a contract, invalid. We have already mentioned the term 'vitiating' and here we will examine the concept in more detail.

The word 'invalid' means that a contract might be rendered void, voidable or unenforceable, and we need to understand the difference between these three terms.

Void contract

A void contract is neither valid nor enforceable. In the eyes of the law, and no matter what the parties may have thought, there never was a contract in the first place. It follows that neither party is bound to perform their obligations under that contract and no legal action can be maintained against them if they fail to do so. A contract compiled over something inherently illegal, e.g. the sale of class A drugs, would be an extreme example of a void contract.

Voidable contract

A voidable contract is a valid and enforceable contract which one party has the right to nullify (or, in legal language, 'avoid'). If they exercise that right, the contract is then void with retrospective effect, as if it had never existed. If they do not exercise that right, the contract remains valid and enforceable.

Unenforceable contract

Normally if a contract is unenforceable, then neither party can maintain a legal action against the other if they fail to perform it. There is really no practical distinction between a contract which is void and a contract which is merely unenforceable.

An example of an unenforceable contract is an agreement to marry, which has been unenforceable since 1971 by Section 1 (1) of the Law Reform (Miscellaneous Provisions) Act 1970. An oral guarantee would be another example. The events that may render a contract void or voidable are:

□   Mistake.

□   Misrepresentation.

□   Duress.

□   Illegality.

Mistake

Mistake can take three forms, as shown below.

Mutual mistake

This occurs when both parties are dealing at cross purposes, and there is genuine confusion about the subject matter of the contract. This would mean that there is no 'consensus ad idem' and the principle is illustrated by the case of *Raffles vs Wichelhaus (1864)*.

Here the buyer agreed to buy some cotton to be transported on the ship 'Peerless'. There were, in fact two ships of that name, one which was sailing in October and the other in December. The buyer believed that he was buying the October shipment whereas the seller believed he was selling the December shipment. The court held that the contract was void due to mistake.

Common mistake

The essential feature about a common mistake is that both parties have made the same mistake about a fundamental feature of the contract and have made an agreement based on a false premise, for example where there is a contract for the sale of some identified goods, which unknown to both parties had perished before the contract was made. The case of *Couturier vs Hastie (1856)* illustrates this principle.

In this case the parties had contracted for the sale of some corn which was in transit aboard ship. Unknown to both parties, a few days before the contract was made, the captain of the ship had sold the corn as it had started to deteriorate and he wished to avoid the loss.

Unilateral mistake

A unilateral mistake occurs when one party has made a mistake about a fundamental facet of the contract with knowledge of the other party. This may arise in two situations:

- a mistake as to the terms of the contract .

- a mistake as to the identity of one of the contracting parties.

When it comes to mistake as to the identity of the other party, there are a number of contradictory cases and theories under this heading. Traditionally, a distinction is made between mistakes as to identity and mistakes as to attributes (e.g. credit worthiness).

A contract is void if the mistaken party intended to do business with another specific person, and the identity of that other person was important to them.

Mistake as to the nature of the document signed

This would be an important area for supply chain specialists. There are two areas to be considered. The first is where a contract has been made in writing, but does not accurately reflect the terms of the agreement. The parties can seek the equitable remedy of rectification to have the document amended to record the agreement accurately.

The second involves what is called in legal jargon, *non est factum* - it is not my deed. There has been little case law to support this, since the decision in *Saunders vs Anglia Building Society (Gallie vs Lee). (1971).*

Here, an old lady was persuaded by her nephew to sign a document conveying her house to her nephew's friend. She had believed she was signing a deed of gift to her nephew. She had not read the document because her glasses were broken. It was held that the document was valid.Before a document will be set aside it must be fundamentally different, in effect, from what it was thought to be and the signatory must prove that he or she had not been negligent in signing the document.

It is also thought that it will only protect a person who is under some disability. The defence did succeed in *Lloyds Bank plc. vs Waterhouse. (1990):*

Here, the defendant, who was illiterate, signed a guarantee of his son's debt to the bank. The father thought that the guarantee covered the purchase price of a farm, but, in fact, it covered all of his son's indebtedness to the bank. It was held that the effect of the document was fundamentally different from what it was believed to be and there was no negligence. The contract was, therefore, void.

Duress and undue influence

We have already considered this, to a great extent, under the Unfair Contract Terms Act. However, we may consider the topic in a little more detail.

Agreement (*consensus ad idem*) assumes the voluntary consent of both contracting parties. Naturally, if the consent of one party is involuntary because their agreement has been induced by duress, the contract should be voidable. What is of more interest to supply chain specialists is economic duress, for instance illegitimate threats to goods, see the case of *Atlas Express Ltd. vs Kafco (Importers and Distributors) Ltd. (1989)*, which we examined earlier.

Economic duress requires:

- Compulsion or coercion of the will, under which heading questions might be, for example:

  - Did the party coerced have an alternative course open to them?

  - Did the party coerced protest?

  - Did the party coerced have independent advice?

  - Did the party take steps to avoid the contract?

  - Illegitimate pressure.

Undue influence

This tends to refer to 'special relationships', such as:

- Parent and child.

- Trustee and beneficiary.

- Solicitor and client.

- Doctor and patient.

- Religious adviser and disciple.

You should note that situations such as these are not really relevant to supply chain specialists and the issue is only included to give as full as picture as possible.

Misrepresentation

It is not only a breach of the terms of a contract which can give rise to legal action.

If a statement made to induce the contract, but which does not become a term of the contract, turns out to be untrue, then the misled party may be able to rescind the contract, or sue for damages.

Material statements made during negotiations leading to a contract may be either:

- Statements which form the express terms of the contract. If these are untrue, the untruth constitutes a breach of contract.

- Statements which do not form part of the contract, but which helped to induce the contract. Such statements are called 'mere representations'. If untrue, they are misrepresentations.

Requirements of misrepresentation

It must be one of the following.

A misrepresentation of fact not of law

Any statement deemed to be misrepresentation must not be any of the following:

- "a mere 'puff'" - that is, a statement so vague as to be without effect, e.g. describing a house as a 'desirable residence' or saying a company has an 'enviable reputation' .

- a promise - a promise to do something in the future is only actionable if the promise amounted to a binding contract.

- a statement of opinion.

- a statement of intention, but if the representor did not have that intention, then it is a mis-statement of fact.

- a statement of law.

A material inducement

A statement will be classed as material if a reasonable person would have been affected by it when deciding whether to enter the contract.

In other words, the misrepresentation must have related to a material fact, rather than a minor or peripheral matter and the plaintiff in any action must show that the statement actually induced them to make the contract.

Remedies for Breach

Buyers have several remedies for breach of contract. These include the following:

- **Rescission** - Putting the parties back to the state they were in at the start of the contract, as if the contract had not taken place (*status quo ante*). For a rescission to be valid, the innocent party must take some positive action although there is no need to contact the other party directly, some action that demonstrates the intention to rescind is all that is necessary. This principle is demonstrated by the case of *Car and Universal Finance Co. Ltd. vs Caldwell (1964)*. This case involved a car obtained by fraudulent misrepresentation, where it was held that the innocent party having informed the police and AA of the fraud was sufficient.

- **Repudiation** - Allowing the plaintiff to avoid the outstanding obligations and liabilities in the contract. A buyer may elect to take this course of action if the seller breaches an implied condition of a contract. If the buyer elects to accept the goods or to treat the breach as a breach of warranty under section 11 of the 1979 Sale of Goods Act, they may claim damages instead.

  You should note that the rules relating to repudiation under the Sale of Goods Act (1979) are rather more complex than this, and if you are in a situation where you might want to invoke these rules, you should consult a dedicated legal textbook.

- **Damages** - Allowing the plaintiff compensation for the effects of a breach.

- **Remedy of specific performance** - Forcing the dilatory party to perform their obligations.

In the event of breach the courts will allow some or all of these remedies depending on the nature of the breach. For instance, as well as a rescission, there may well be a damages claim for the loss caused to the innocent rescinding party by the other party to the contract.

You should note the following:

- For breaches of terms deemed to be warranties, as opposed to conditions (see earlier in the chapter) you can only sue for damages.

☐ For breaches of terms deemed to be conditions, you may sue for rescission, repudiation, damages, and specific performance, although you should note that specific performance actions are mutually exclusive to repudiation and rescission actions.

The last point, about the distinction between breaches of warranties and breaches of conditions, is an over-simplification. The crucial question is usually, 'What is meant by a serious breach?' How, in practice, can a serious breach be distinguished from a minor one? Some of the case law is confusing. Some seem to follow the traditional approach of 'conditions' and 'warranties'.

Other cases suggest that the wronged party has the right to terminate if the breach 'goes to the root of the contract', or else if the breach deprives them of the whole or a significant part of the benefit they would have gained from performance.

Generally, each particular case must be considered on its own facts, including the relative importance of the term which is broken, the nature of the breach, and the severity of the consequences for the wronged party.

Definition of damages

It is important here to discuss, in some depth, some areas which are generally and often abused in contractual terms, and cause buyers a great deal of confusion.

Liquidated damages

Parties to a contract may stipulate in the contract that, in the event of a breach, the damages shall be a certain sum or calculated in a specified way. If the sum represents a genuine attempt to pre-estimate the loss, then it will be enforced by the court as liquidated damages, even if it turns out to be inaccurate.

In *Cellulose Acetate Silk Co. vs Widnes Foundry Ltd. (1925)*, damages were set in the contract at £20 per working week, in the event of a delay in performance. There was a delay of 30 weeks, and the loss to the plaintiff was £5 850. It was held that the liquidated damages of 30 weeks x £20, i.e. £600, would be enforced.

Liquidated damages must be distinguished from:

☐ Exemption clauses limiting liability:

• These fix the maximum sum recoverable. If the actual loss is less, then only the lesser sum may be recovered.

☐ Penalty clauses.

Penalty clauses

These are not genuine attempts to pre-estimate the loss, but are designed to frighten the other party into performing the contract, or to punish them. The use of the words 'penalty' or 'liquidated damages' is not conclusive. Whether a sum is a penalty or liquidated damages is a matter of construction, and the following guidelines have come from case law. A clause is deemed to be a penalty:

☐   If the sum is extravagant and unconscionable.

☐   If a larger sum is payable on the failure to pay a smaller sum.

☐   If the same sum is payable on major and minor breaches.

☐   If it is no obstacle to the sum being liquidated that a precise pre-estimate is almost impossible.

Penalty clauses will not be enforced by the court. Instead, the court may award 'unliquidated' damages. The rule against penalties does not apply to:

☐   **Acceleration clauses:** Quite often, in contracts, the terms will include some sort of reward or bonus to the other party if they complete the work in a specified time period which is less than the original envisaged time. Here, the whole of a debt becomes payable immediately if certain conditions are not observed.

☐   **Deposits:** These are guarantees that contracts will be performed (these must be distinguished from part-payments).

☐   Payments on events other than a breach of contract.

☐   Clauses stipulating that a term is a condition. Companies will, therefore, generally use one of the four devices above in their wording.

'Unliquidated' damages

The purpose of unliquidated damages is to compensate the plaintiff for loss suffered as a result of a breach. The purpose is not:

☐   To punish the defendant. Punitive damages are not awarded for breach of contract.

☐   To recoup a gain made by the defendant. Damages are assessed on the loss to the plaintiff, not on the gain to the defendant. If the plaintiff has not suffered a loss, then nominal damages only will be awarded.

Generally, where there is no agreed figure for the damages, the plaintiff will sue for 'unliquidated' damages, this being the sum that the court considers appropriate to compensate the injured party for the loss that they have suffered as a result of the breach. If no loss has been sustained, the court will award nominal damages to acknowledge the breach.

To be recoverable, the damages must relate to loss that was foreseeable at the time that the contract was made. The case that established this principle was *Hadley vs Baxendale (1854)*.

In this case, the plaintiff mill-owner employed the defendant to transport a broken crankshaft to the shaft manufacturer to enable it to be used as a pattern for the construction of a new replacement part. The defendant negligently delayed delivery of the shaft resulting in the mill being closed longer than would otherwise have been the case.

The plaintiff sued for his loss of profits due to the mill being out of use. The court held that the defendant was not liable as there was nothing to suggest that he should have been aware of the special losses that the plaintiff would suffer as a result of the delay. The plaintiff might have had a spare shaft. The rules emanating from the Hadley decision mean that recoverable damage is limited to that which falls within two specified criteria:

- such damage as arises naturally from the breach, i.e. in the usual course of events.

- such damage that, while not arising naturally, 'may reasonably be supposed to have been in the contemplation of both parties at the time they made the contract' as being the probable result of the breach.

Applying these rules, it follows that the defendant in the *Hadley vs Baxendale* decision would have been liable for the plaintiff's loss of profits if he had known that the plaintiff did not have a spare shaft and thus that any delay would cause increased damage.

How are damages assessed?

This is a very difficult question to answer in short, and there is a plethora of complicated case law. However, damages for breach are supposed to place the injured party in the position they would have been in had the breach not occurred.
This is generally assessed in two ways:

- Loss of profit calculations.

- Reliance losses where the costs incurred by the injured party in reliance that the contract would be performed are calculated and recovered.

Consequential costs or remoteness of damage

Situations can arise where a breach of contract leads to not only a loss immediately attributable to the breach but to other further consequences which then give rise to other additional or consequential losses. Can buyers recover for these consequential losses? The rules for determining what losses could and could not be claimed are laid down in the case of Hadley and Baxendale (1854) described above.

These principles have now been developed as follows:

Where a contract has been breached, the damages in respect of the breach should be such as may have fairly and reasonably be considered either as arising naturally, i.e. according to the usual course of things, from such a breach of contract itself, or such as may reasonably be supposed to have been in the contemplation of both parties, at the time they made the contract, as the probable result of the breach of it.

Actual knowledge

Defendants' knowledge of special circumstances that could result in losses, must be precise. This encourages contracting parties to disclose clearly any exceptional losses in advance.

Types of loss recognised

Case law is growing all the time, recording instances of success in claiming remote or consequential loss. Generally, so far, the following types of loss are recognised:

- Pecuniary loss.

- Pain and suffering consequent on physical injury.

- Physical inconvenience. In *Watts vs Morrow (1991)*, damages were awarded for the physical inconvenience of living in a house whilst repairs were being carried out.

- Damage to commercial reputation. In *Gibbons vs Westminster Bank (1939)*, damages for the injury to his reputation were awarded to a trader whose cheque was wrongly dishonoured.

☐ Distress to plaintiff. In *Jarvis vs Swan Tours (1973)*, damages for disappointment were awarded against a tour operator who provided a holiday that did not correspond with its description. It has been suggested that damages for distress are particularly in consumer goods contracts. However, for the buyer working for an organisation manufacturing consumer goods, they should be vigilant on how they protect the quality of their goods, and their commercial dealings with their suppliers.

☐ Distress to third parties. *Jackson vs Horizon Holidays Ltd. (1975).* Here, the plaintiff entered into a contract with a holiday firm for a holiday for his family and himself in Ceylon (Sri Lanka). The holiday was a disaster. The plaintiff recovered damages for £500 for 'mental stress'. On appeal, the court confirmed the amount on the grounds that witnessing the distress of his own family had increased the plaintiff's own distress.

☐ Speculative damage. The fact that damages are difficult to assess will not normally prevent the court from making an assessment. In *Chaplin vs Hicks (1917)*, the plaintiff recovered damages for loss of a chance to take part in a beauty contest.

For buyers, all of this means that they need to define very carefully what they contemplate as the results of a breach and agree these with the sellers at the time of making the contract. Often this will result in sellers wishing to include a contract clause limiting their liabilities to a maximum value and will require negotiation in order to agree on such liabilities.

Chapter Summary

As was mentioned at the beginning of this chapter, the intention here has been to provide the basics, the 'bare bones', of law relating to purchasing and supply, particularly that part of the law relating to contract.

The law is an extremely complex and difficult subject and just when you feel that you have mastered a particular aspect of it, you find an exception to the basic principle, which only serves to confuse matters further.

However, the information contained in this chapter should provide you with the essentials required to be able to deal with legal issues at Foundation/level 4 of your CIPS studies.

BIBLIOGRAPHY

'Purchasing and Supply Chain Management'. 2006. K. Lysons and B. Farrington. (FT Prentice Hall).

'Purchasing Principles and Management'. 2005. Baily, Farmer, Jessop and Jones. (FT Prentice Hall).

'One Stop Contracts'. 2000. John Wyborn. (ICSA).

'Integrated Materials Management'. 1993. R.J.Carter and P.M.Price. (Pitman Publishing).

'Stores and Distribution Management'. 2005. R.J.Carter, P.M.Price and S.A.Emmett. (Liverpool Business Publishing).

INDEX